THE
WORK
OF
HOPE

HOW INDIVIDUALS & ORGANIZATIONS
CAN AUTHENTICALLY DO GOOD

Richard C. Harwood

**KETTERING
FOUNDATION
PRESS**

To Mom and Dad—who did the work of my hope
everyday in our community

© 2012 by the Charles F. Kettering Foundation

ALL RIGHTS RESERVED.

For information about permission to reproduce
selections from this book, write to:
Permissions
Kettering Foundation Press
200 Commons Road
Dayton, Ohio 45459

First Edition, 2012

Manufactured in the United States of America

Cover photograph by Mathew Septimus
Design by Tronvig Group

Library of Congress Cataloging-in-Publication-Data
The Work of Hope: How Individuals and Organizations Can Authentically Do Good
p. cm
ISBN: 978-0 923993-45-0
Library of Congress Control Number: 2012944016

CONTENTS

FOREWORD

David Mathews

The Kettering Foundation's collaboration with Rich Harwood and his associates has been quite productive over the years. This has been due, in no small part, to Rich's keen eye for deciphering the American psyche. His 1991 study, *Citizens and Politics: A View from Main Street America*, showed that what was then thought to be an apathetic public was actually a very angry citizenry. Harwood's research went beneath the usual dissatisfaction with government and politicians to reveal people's strong feelings about powerlessness and exclusion, coupled with an untapped sense of civic duty. According to the study, no interpretation of the public is less accurate than the often-repeated contention that people are consumed with their own private lives. Those who participated in the study were far from being civically detached. In fact, they cared so deeply about the future of our democracy that their frustration fueled cynicism—a cynicism they worried about passing on to their children. Americans felt they had been pushed out of the political system by a professional class of powerful lobbyists, incumbent politicians, campaign managers—and a media elite. They saw a system in which money ruled; a system with its doors closed to the average citizen.

Today, numerous studies report a dramatic loss of public confidence, not only in the government and the political system, but also in most other institutions like schools, nongovernmental organizations, and businesses to name just three. And this loss engulfs nearly all the world's industrialized democracies, not just the United States. These studies also usefully distinguish between confidence in politicians (who are lightning rods for public blame) and confidence in the institutions themselves. This loss of confidence, initially attributed to unsettling circumstances like changes in economic conditions, now seems related to other factors such as citizens' greater expectations of institutions, which they have become more dependent upon for assistance even as they have grown more distrustful.

Since the 1991 Main Street study, the foundation has learned that when people are confronted with specific issues, their perceptions of institutions evolve; stereotypes give way to specific experiences. Deliberative forums on contentious issues like health care and the national debt obviously implicate institutions like hospitals and government agencies. And deliberation encourages citizens to do more than make wish lists and complain. They have to confront the tensions that occur when some of the things they value require sacrificing other things they hold dear. They also have to decide which institutions are best suited to different tasks—and what they themselves are willing to do. To follow up on this insight, Kettering asked the Harwood Institute to join us in probing deeper into people's attitudes—with particular attention to what citizens have to say about correcting what they don't like.

Kettering entered into this research with particular questions in mind. Do citizens just want more efficient and effective institutions? Or do they want more control in their own hands to shape a future they find increasingly dangerous and uncertain? Many people appear to feel the way folks feel when the remote to their TV no longer controls the set. The battery appears to be dead or some kind of "bug" has invaded the electronics. You can hear their consternation in comments like, "the system is out of whack" and "the rules have changed (and I don't know what they are anymore)." Having institutions assure them that they will take care of the problems may not be enough.

This Harwood study didn't disappoint us. It uncovers the values that are driving both the public's hopes and fears. Americans haven't given up on the country; they think we have the DNA for resilience in our bones. They believe, however, that we have lost our way because we've misplaced our moral compass. We are irrepressible shoppers who have been taken over by materialism. Wall Street is a convenient symbol for the greed people see everywhere. The citizens Harwood talked to think Americans have too little compassion for one another and too little regard for the dignity of others.

How do we find our way to where we want America to be? Grand visions and systemic reforms, Harwood finds, aren't as credible as small projects where citizens set the goals and do the work themselves. This homegrown change is appealing because it is authentic and incremental. Unsure that they can trust large institutions, people look to their fellow citizens to fix what is out of whack, using cooperative efforts that build trust. In one of the most telling examples in this research, neighbors who talked about coming together to paint a school didn't want to do it just to make the building more attractive; they valued the painting as a tangible demonstration of what can be accomplished when citizens work together. People have been improving community buildings for a long time, but in this case, that wasn't the primary objective. The purpose was to show that citizens can get a greater measure of control by combining their energies. That was a way they could get more power in their hands.

The story of people joining forces to paint suggests that Americans may be moving beyond their expectations of institutions to look at their expectations of *themselves*. However, despite examples of collaborative problem solving, citizens continue to be depicted in many publications as apathetic "couch potatoes" living in isolated enclaves—getting up only to protect themselves and perhaps a few close friends. We have all heard numerous accounts of how self-centered people can be—how they are narrowly focused and indifferent to the good of all.

Although people can be quite self-protective, the foundation has seen evidence that they aren't as much unwilling to join forces with other citizens as they are plagued by uncertainties. Voices across the country interact as though people were speaking in a contemporary play about the role of citizens. In Act I, the opening line is from a man from Minnesota who says confidently, "I think there's a hunger for engagement, generally, with people." He then adds a caveat, "I think they're just looking for ways to be engaged." Not persuaded, a woman from Idaho counters, "When I told the citizens I worked with that they have more power than they believed, I think I believed it when I said it. And I believed it all the times that I lived it. But I'm not sure it's as true as it used to be." Trying to reconcile the two perceptions, a woman from Rhode Island reasons that, "people … do care; they just don't know what to do with themselves."

The Harwood study takes us to Act II, which helps us understand more fully what is being said in this civic drama. The study shows that while criticizing institutions for their failures is rampant, Americans aren't sure citizens are holding up their end of the responsibilities for the future either. Nonetheless, being pragmatic, people realize they have no choice but to try to work together—and perhaps with their institutions. They recognize that "me" and "us" are interdependent. This may be the most important finding of all in this insightful study.

AUTHOR'S PREFACE

About This Book

The Kettering Foundation and Harwood Institute for Public Innovation have long been interested in the health of democracy and people's engagement in public and community life. As David Mathews observed in his Foreword, some 20 years ago, in one of our early studies together, the Kettering Foundation commissioned the Harwood Institute (then The Harwood Group) to explore the relationship between citizens and politics and people's lives.

Now, on the 20th anniversary of that initial study—*Citizens and Politics: A View from Main Street America*—the two organizations wanted to know how the country has evolved, over these past two decades. During this time the nation has experienced rapid and significant change—from the largest peace-time economic expansion in American history to the Great Recession; from the September 11 attacks on our own soil to two ongoing wars overseas; from people's acute anger about politics to their troubling concerns about their own lives and the life of the nation, to mention only a few of the most dismaying events. In comparison to the insights we discovered in 1991, we wanted to know exactly how people see their lives today, so we decided once again to explore with people the following issues:

- How are things going in the country today?
- What are people's chief concerns?
- How do people feel about politics today, and why?
- To what extent do people feel they can make a difference in how things go or turn out in the country, in their own lives?
- Whom do people trust and what is the nature of the relationship?
- What would give people confidence that things are on the right track?

To do this, my colleagues and I, over the course of about a year, have taken a "long walk" across the country, engaging a representative cross-section of Americans in deep, three-hour conversations. Each conversation was made up of 12-15 individuals. There were 11 conversations conducted in all, held in communities across the nation: Detroit, Michigan; Champaign-Urbana, Illinois; Sonoma, California; Bend, Oregon; Jacksonville, Florida; Las Vegas, Nevada; New York, New York; Dallas, Texas; Nashville, Tennessee; Baltimore, Maryland; and Denver, Colorado.

Such lengthy and open discussions are particularly well-suited for this type of study; they allow people to express not only *what* they think—but also *why* and *how* their views came about. This type of insight is impossible to gather through public opinion surveys. In surveys, for instance, questions largely need to be predefined for people to answer in only seconds; the respondents are unable to explore, or discuss with others, various related topics, issues, and concerns that may be connected to the survey question and may be of utmost importance to them. They are unable then to reconsider or expound upon their own views. And only a limited amount of new information can be entered into the discussion for people to consider.

All this said, I must still point out that the observations drawn from the group discussions in this book need to be viewed, strictly speaking, as hypotheses that should be verified by scientifically reliable methods in order to consider them definitive. More information about the methodology used for this study is found in the Appendix.

My intention in writing this book was not to list one-by-one, a set of individual, even fragmented findings. That approach would have missed the essence of what we discovered was on people's minds. For Americans are engaged in a struggle about the direction of their lives and the lives of their communities and this nation. They are trying to piece together a host of cross-currents from an array of directions and sources to make sense of what's happening around them. They long to understand the meaning of these cross-currents: what do they add up to?, what do they imply about our individual and collective futures?, and how can they be acted upon? Indeed, a point-by-point recitation of findings would deny people a sense of possibility of what it will take to move ahead.

Thus, my role in this book is not only to report what I heard, but also to explain to the best of my ability where we are as a nation and how we might move ahead. In this way, the task is to shed light from what we learned and to discuss how we might cope with current conditions, even how people and the nation might forge a new path forward. Think of this book as a reflection of travels across the country, listening deeply to people and, then, pulling together not only what was heard, but a larger narrative, its meaning, and its implications.

I bring to this book, of course, previous efforts and experiences that help to provide context—such as the earlier books (*Citizens and Politics: A View from Main Street America*; *Hope Unraveled: The People's Retreat and Our Way Back*) and numerous studies about the condition of the country in different times—in all of which I sought to aid individuals, organizations, and communities to counter some of the prevailing forces facing them—and to shape their own futures. Broadly speaking, this book uses this foundation of knowledge and experience as a way of drawing out the meaning of what we have heard in the past year.

Many people who will read this book already sense that the nation is undergoing great change and tumult; they yearn to place the country on a new path forward. Our hope is that this book will help them and others make sense of where we are, understand some of the reasons for how we got here, and determine how we might, together, move ahead.

1

WHERE WE ARE TODAY

A look at our first Main Street study, *Citizens and Politics: A View from Main Street America*, is perhaps the best way to introduce the radically different findings of this new Main Street study. In 1991, the nation's political system and its many failings dominated our conversations with Americans across the country. Today, the conversations are radically changed. The currency of our time is no longer politics—but people, their lives, and their everyday concerns. It is, ultimately, about what it means to move forward *together*, to restore a sense of faith in ourselves and in one another.

Our initial Main Street report was among the first in the nation to reveal that Americans were *not* apathetic about politics and public life—as conventional wisdom had insisted—but instead felt pushed out, disconnected, and impotent. The public hadn't rejected politics.

In effect, people felt that politics had rejected them. At the time, Americans complained bitterly about a system made up of politicians, news media, and special interests that had overtaken what I refer to as the public square and operated with little regard for the people who lived and worked within it.

Ironically, this sense of disconnection, and the unmitigated anger that accompanied it, was bubbling up in the nation just as the United States was celebrating victory in the first Gulf War, a wave of patriotism was sweeping the country, and President George H.W. Bush was enjoying sky-high approval ratings. Still, amid the celebrations and hoopla, our discussions with people indicated that something was terribly wrong in the body politic: people's deep anger had not abated, nor would it.

America must "think anew about politics if we are to improve our political health," I wrote in the first Main Street study. The recommendations we put forward based on those discussions focused on the urgent need to find more and better ways to shift the political debate towards issues people cared about. We argued for citizens to form a public voice on policy issues to counteract the voices of powerful special interests. And we believed there must be more effective ways for citizens and public officials to interact more constructively. What we proposed sought to change the workings of politics and find a place for citizens within it.

All this is part of the past.

What we learned in this new study is that politics and people's disgust with it is no longer the central, dominant narrative in America. Now the endless, often mind-numbing churn of politics lives outside people's everyday world—operating as if in an entirely separate universe, with its own set of rules, winners and losers, and purpose. The fact is, people barely mentioned it, relatively speaking. Their chief concerns are elsewhere.

In recent years, the country has endured the largest economic downturn since the Great Depression, two wars, and enough acrimony and divisiveness to virtually grind our public discourse and collective efforts to a halt. Along the way, Barack Obama was elected president, and many people thought—*wished*—his election would signify a positive transformational turn in our politics and public life. Since then, outrage has boiled over in the form of the right-leaning "Tea Party" and the left-leaning "Occupy Wall Street," among other protests, movements, and initiatives that seek to organize Americans into battalions of anger.

In our new discussions with Americans across the country we learned that people have been left bereft of a sense of possibility. We learned that people condemn our individual and collective inability to come together to get things done. And they are exhausted by the public recriminations and acrimony that hold our discourse hostage. There is palpable fear among them over their ever-increasing sense of isolation from one another. At the heart of these

People are bereft of a sense of possibility.

feelings is the deep sense—the belief—that current conditions in America actively undermine much of what is good and right in our in society—and in our very selves. And in many respects, people say they have had a hand in bringing about some of these conditions.

People believe we can do better. There is a yearning within them to come back into the public square to engage *with one another*, to find ways to get things done *together*, and to restore their belief in themselves and their fellow citizens. Put another way, what people are telling us about is a desire to reclaim a sense of humanity and to tap the innate goodness and potential that resides within each of us. As they see it, only then can the negative conditions now shaping the nation be fought and, ultimately, altered.

The good news is that people are ready to step forward, if the conditions are right.

A RADICAL SHIFT OVER 20 YEARS	
In 1991 People Felt:	In 2012 People Feel:
Unmitigated anger about politics and the political system—including politicians, news media, and special interests	A deep concern about people, their lives, and their daily concerns. Politics largely irrelevant
Pushed out of politics—disconnected, impotent	Bereft of a sense of possibility about their lives and the life of the country
A lack of trust	An absence of trust
An urge to be heard in politics and the political *system*	Yearning to get back to basics—to ignite compassion, openness and humility, and concern for the common good, in *daily life*
Existing troubles in political system could be "fixed"	Solution is to kick-start a new path—a way forward—for people and the country
Disconnect between their local civic actions and politics and political system	To put country on right track, people must come together to get things done—on a *human scale*
"Throw the bums out" as the prevailing mood	They must tap their innate goodness and potential as key source for progress
Restoration of belief in political leaders and the political system was essential	A need to restore people's belief in themselves and in one another

OUR WAY HOME

If 1991 was about the *political system*, then 2012 is about something more distinctly *human*. The Americans with whom we've been speaking long to pierce through the noise enveloping their lives and society-at-large, to get back to basics regarding what is most important and vital in life. Their desire is to return to first principles. They long to put America on a different trajectory, a new path. Based on these conversations, I believe there are three guideposts for moving forward, which I briefly describe here:

- **Our sense of humanity**. Present-day conditions too often leave little room for people's aspirations and the values they care about. Instead, people and their lives are sidelined, squeezed out, even stripped out of how American life operates. Now people insist we must focus on making room for genuine human interactions and for people to express and make real their basic human yearnings and hopes.

- **Getting things done together**. We live in a time when progress can seem impossible and gridlock is our default posture. Now Americans want to find ways to come together, set goals, achieve them, and build from there.

- **Restoration of belief in ourselves and in one another**. Much of what happens in the public square today is that we push ourselves apart from one another, place blame for our failings, and cast aspersions. "Belief" is the new currency of change—the belief that we can act together and that we have the ability, know-how, and wisdom to do so. There is no silver bullet to achieve this.

Listening closely to Americans, we find that they do not express a desire for political leaders to fix problems *for* them. Nor do they expect some large foundation, organization, or other group single-handedly to lead the way to hopefulness and a more humane life (as if they, alone, knew the way). They do not complain endlessly about the short-comings of others, as they did in 1991. More often people see themselves as the critical actors in righting the nation and their lives today.

They are clear that to move in a new direction—down a new path—will require getting back to enduring values people have long cherished and which now must guide the country in moving forward. The values they point to include: *compassion*—the need for people once again to see and hear each other, reach out to the other, and support each other; the *importance of children*—viewed as a gauge of the very health of our society, and the basis upon which to build the future; *openness and humility*—the room to engage with others, listen attentively, discern what may be truly important, and thus act with care; and concern for *the common good*—to believe, at a time when people are implored daily to think solely about their own survival, their own good, that we hold *shared* interests.

Yet as promising and as essential as these enduring values are, people also want to identify *practical* ways to get things moving—to put the values into motion and create a different dynamic in their own lives, in their communities, and in the nation as a whole. Through these discussions it becomes apparent that people seek to kick-start a new trajectory—a new direction for the country, a new sense of hope and possibility. They do not believe this will happen overnight; nor do they imagine that it will come from a series of large, grand new initiatives or policies, for many people no doubt would question the veracity and reliability of such efforts. This new trajectory, people say, will take shape only through actions that start small, and local, between and among them, beginning close to home, on a human scale. In this way, people coming out from their homes can start to rebuild trust. They can both set goals and achieve them. They can restore belief in themselves and in one another.

Still, those Americans we spoke with are clear that even these actions, whatever form they may take, would not alone be enough to solve our most pressing challenges. Rather, the true power of such actions is in signaling to ourselves and others what is possible. It is to make an entreaty, as it were, to fellow Americans to come back into the public square. What people want is to engender an ever-growing ripple effect in the nation that in turn will lead to forging new and more productive norms in the public square.

The reasons for this close-to-home, small-scale approach are clear. The nation is stuck, stymied. Too few openings seem available for positive movement. Various leaders and organizations appear to lack a desire and willingness to get things done together. And people remain anxious and uncertain about their future while mistrust abounds. What people seem to be saying is that this new trajectory can serve as a counterforce to business-as-usual, initiating actions from *outside* the current system. People believe this is how we must start to change the country's direction. They believe that these actions, taken together, can produce a disruption, a jolt to the system itself. And it is through these ever-expanding, locally grown actions that people can tap into and rediscover their own innate power and potential to shape their environment and find greater control over their lives and their future.

Let's be clear: this is not to say that changes from *within* the system are not needed or valued. Only that people are not holding their breath for such changes to come about and for any such changes to be effective. What this adds up to is a radical departure from what people said in 1991: the focus is now on people creating action from outside the political system rather than working entirely from the inside.

The good news in this regard is that all across the country, in communities large and small, many promising pockets of change already have taken root and are flourishing, while many others are starting each and every day. While this is not the place to catalogue these many pockets of change, it is possible to say what they often hold in common. They provide room for people to act on their aspirations (as opposed to their primary complaints and claims) for their community. They enable people to come together and make choices about how they can take action, together. They help to align organizations and institutions—together with everyday people—in ways that bring about effective collective action. Such efforts take place on a host of issues and concerns and can actively be built upon in creating a new trajectory.

CONVENTIONAL WISDOM AND ITS TRAPS

Before we go any further in pursuing what this new Main Street study tells us about America, an important warning is in order. We need to be on guard against conventional wisdom, which today, as always, offers its own ways about how to move the country forward. A few moments of reflection show that these conventional ways often bear little relationship to people reclaiming a sense of humanity, restoring their belief in themselves and others, and getting things done together. In fact, just the opposite can be true: the worn path of conventional wisdom can exac-erbate—*deepen*—the very maladies we seek to overcome. Conventional wisdom, left unexamined and un-checked, tends to keep us on the same old path that people like those we talked with in this new study so desperately want to escape.

Conventional wisdom, left unexamined and unchecked, tends to keep us on the same old path that people so desperately want to escape.

Consider these examples of what conventional wisdom urges us to do—all of which we must avoid:

- Turn up the volume of acrimony and divisiveness as a meth-od to mobilize supporters and drown out—or overwhelm—opponents in order to win for our side;

- Launch yet another new program, initiative, or policy, only this time make it bigger, with more public relations punch, and based on promises to change the world;

- Organize people to express their outrage and make de-mands—to push, push, *and* push! (But what happens after the outrage?)

- Raise more money in order to do more—but toward what end?

- Tap the power of the Internet to get people to donate money and engage in support for a cause—as if these actions alone will meet people's true desire to reengage and reconnect;

- Pursue the magic bullet of some legislative fix, or pursue the perfect candidate, as if such pursuits on their own will be enough;

- Create mechanized approaches to be more efficient in engaging people and more productive in scaling efforts—but without reference to people's sense of humanity?

Any of these steps may very well enable some individuals, political parties, and other interested groups to win an election, a policy debate, or appeal to more new members or supporters for their cause. They may result in greater attention for one point-of-view or another. They may spur more people to donate money. Even the various nonprofits, foundations, and neighborhood groups, among other groups that expressly make their mission the well-being of communities and society-writ-large increasingly adopt these approaches. Sometimes such efforts are wrapped in more palatable language, strategies, and taglines, but nonetheless they are guided by the same underlying assumptions of conventional wisdom. Such assumptions will change nothing fundamental and will keep alive the blockades that prevent us from finding the new ways of joining together. Such steps will not address people's deepest yearnings.

Nor will these conventional responses address a set of deeper challenges that have been taking shape for years, which are not only harmful now, but also are part of a more complicated story than outlined thus far, and that must be fully understood and addressed in order to move forward. Each of these deeper challenges will be addressed in later chapters but are worth noting here. Among them is the triumph of consumerism in the United States, the likes of which make us an impulsive society, where instant gratification is the expectation, and thinking about being part of something larger than ourselves can seem beyond our reach. There is a pervasive absence of trust in leaders and organizations of all kinds, at all levels, in society, including at times, as we shall see, those individuals closest to us in our own lives. There are, people say, a set of rigged rules that favor the wealthy and powerful and "connected," which have led many to believe the American Dream is no longer possible, and so leaves them with little recourse. People worry that what I call "a broken moral compass" continually leads them and the country down the wrong path—when we already know the right thing to do.

These challenges have come to circumscribe people's lives—shaping what they do in everyday life, what they have come to believe in, and what it means to move forward from here. Maybe for years these challenges have nagged and pulled at us, trying to grab our full attention; now they're center stage. They strike directly at how we see ourselves and who we will be. The challenges must be addressed, people say, if they are to put themselves and the nation on a better course. And yet we must know that these deeper challenges make the course ahead more difficult, more divisive.

Now here is a quick overview of the new path ahead.

A NEW PATH

What we hear in the words of the people quoted in *The Work of Hope*—hear in their dismay and in their longings for another way—indicates that to move forward will require that we come to grips with the challenges that face us. We must be willing to see them and to engage with them. We must turn toward them, not turn away from them. I believe that Americans are ready to do this—they see no other option.

And what I report on in *The Work of Hope* also tells us we must turn our attention to the underlying conditions that can place us

The greatest risk at hand is that we fail to reclaim and build the necessary space for genuine human interactions to occur, for people to come together, for the seeds of belief to be nurtured and grown.

on a better path. It is these conditions that are the very ingredients that make society and people's lives work. Thus, at this juncture in the nation's journey we must not let slip from our minds—from our very line of sight—what it means to make room for people to exercise their deepest yearnings, to make them real, to bring them to life. The greatest risk at hand is that we fail to reclaim *and* fail to build the necessary space for genuine human interactions to occur, for people to come together, for the seeds of belief to be nurtured and grown.

In the pages that follow you will hear people talk about their lives and this nation. As I have listened closely to their voices and placed them in the broader context of my more than 25 years of work; I am struck by what they suggest. Surely, there are any number of ways to move forward from here, but I ask you to focus on the following five elements. They are not offered, singly or together, as any kind of a silver bullet. Nor are they intended to be comprehensive. Rather, they provide a starting point, a way for us to place people, their lives, and the life of the nation on a different path forward.

First, we must make the necessary room for people to come back into the public square in ways that will enable them to actually interact, build trust. We must avoid succumbing to fast and easy ways of engagement that merely ask people to donate from the comforts of their home, or plug-in for quickie volunteering experiences in which they have little real interaction with others, and the like. Such efforts can produce laudable benefits in the short run, but they do not answer people's deep yearnings to come together.

Second, we must produce opportunities for people to act on a human scale. Small and local is where people want to start—where they can regain their footing, their confidence, and do things together. People want to see and drive such actions, and enlarge them, moving forward. We must beware of simply engaging people in someone else's journey—in some other group's pre-set goals and plans—where no room exists for genuine actions driven by individual citizens.

Third, we must be ever-vigilant in how we approach this path forward. It is all too easy to adopt the right words—*compassion, openness, humility,* and the *common good*—yet not experience their true meaning. We must create in various initiatives and efforts—in our own daily lives—room for these enduring values to be exercised and to flourish. The question to ask is: How can we make genuine room for these values in our daily lives and work? The impulse always is to say they *are* present in our work—to give ourselves a good grade—when they are present in name only.

Fourth, to repeat themes from previous elements, we must make the necessary room for people to come back into the public square so that they are actually working *together*, on a human scale, where real room exists to exercise compassion, openness, humility, and the common good. For all these must be tended to if collective action is to succeed. Without this underlying foundation, we cannot create the necessary public will, the public discourse that can produce it, and the marshalling of individual and collective resources that are required to move ahead effectively. Set apart from this essential foundation, collective action runs the risk of becoming merely an exercise in moving around existing ways of doing things in communities, without paying attention to what matters most to people. That is a recipe merely to continue down the worn path we seek to change.

Fifth, and finally, we must know that change won't come all at once. It never has. So as people and groups build ever-expanding efforts at change, we must pay special attention to creating a new narrative about being on a better course, one that offers people authentic hope and possibility. This happens only when people can see how a larger story is unfolding over time—how one example of action, or "proof point," connects to many others, and then to another! Such proof points are less about, say, a single organization's triumph—its record-setting fundraising or its own narrow metrics—but about people, their lives, and their concerns.

What we have come to know in this new set of conversations across America is that our main task today is to make room within people's lives *and* the larger society for a greater sense of humanity to take hold and guide us. It is for us to act on a more human scale, where people can start close to home, and exercise greater control. It is to find new and better ways to insert into our lives a greater degree of compassion, openness, humility, and concern for the common good. And it demands nothing less than to restore people's belief in themselves and one another.

This is the new path.

2

THE TOWER OF BABEL

Have you ever experienced a time in your life when you sensed something critical had gone awry while all the people around you—many of whom say they want to help—just keep talking *at* you? Over time, they may raise their voices, even shout at you, perhaps to try to make you feel guilty—all to gain your attention, persuade you to adopt a certain point-of-view, and court you to take action according to *their* wishes. At times what they say may matter little to your own concerns, or even offend you, prompting you to cover your ears or eyes to get away from the noise.

This is how many Americans feel about public discourse today and their interactions in public life, even when the discourse seems to offer promises for moving the country forward. We live in a persistent state of noise that is crippling our efforts to create the communities, the country, and the lives we want. One of the first comments my colleagues and I heard in our conversations across the country came from a Las Vegas woman who named perfectly the sense of harsh noise that marks much of our public discussion:

> To me, this country is like the Tower of Babel, meaning that everybody is speaking different languages and it's all chaotic. And if you can't work together, then it's going to be chaos. And [we] can't! So everybody divides and goes to their own different sides and creates their own different things. And people suffer from it. So it's chaotic, divided. We're just the Tower of Babel.

In this Tower of Babel people feel stuck; there's no apparent place for them to go where some greater sense of possibility for the future can be heard. They worry that present day conditions are undermining much of what is good in our society and in them. A Detroit woman said, "I just feel like there's no hope. I'm scared. I'm scared for me. I'm scared for my son." A Las Vegas woman echoed dramatically the thoughts and sentiments of many discussion participants:

In this Tower of Babel people feel stuck; there's no apparent place for them to go where some greater sense of possibility for the future can be heard.

> Things have come undone. I'm 65 years old, and I never thought I'd say today that I was glad I didn't have grandchildren. I'm glad I don't have grandchildren because I hate to see what we're going to have in this country in another 10, 20 years.

No doubt that at the core of these trying times in recent years has been the nation's struggling economy; and as it improves, one certainly hopes people's sense of the future will brighten. But in listening closely to Americans, one hears mostly about the noise and its effects—for instance, about the inability of people, on different sides of issues, to come together; about endless public recriminations and acrimony; about people's sense that in their own lives they are failing to do what is good and right; and about the now flagging hope that the nation might sometime get to the essence of its challenges. These are matters that go to people's deeper concerns about their own lives, their future. They question the extent to which they can regain a sense of control and hope. One Dallas man put it like this: "We've got a struggling economy, and it seems like we're off course ... so everybody's blaming everybody else." He then continued, "It seems like we can't get to the bottom of the problem and work it out."

What happens when it seems nearly impossible to confront the problems that beset communities and the nation? What happens when people see few improvements on the horizon that address the core challenges that directly affect their everyday lives? Here's how one Champaign man sees it:

> I think people are increasingly worried, not only about this economic crisis, but also about whether the country is in a position to be dealing with it—whether this country is governable. There's a sort of political paralysis. There's an increasing amount of division between different groups. And I think the frustration is not only with the state the country is in, but also with its inability to respond to the challenges it's facing.

Of course, there are many "solutions" being proposed to deal with our current challenges. But simply pushing more large-scale initiatives, sophisticated plans to reform politics, or searches for perfect candidates for leadership (among other possible "solutions") will not do. Many of these efforts may be sound; no doubt they are. But it is clear from the people we met across the country that the challenges we face are more fundamental, more human, and much more provocative. They require something more.

I said this before, and repeat it here deliberately: At issue is whether people will come back into the public square to engage with one another, to solve problems together, and to find a way to believe in themselves and others. At issue is whether basic levels of trust can be re-established. These matters are the very ingredients required for communities and the country to work. Without a focus on these matters, the ability to effectively address knotty and longstanding issues, such as the economy or public schools, or any other large-scale concern, will be stymied.

During our recent conversations across the nation, we asked people to offer up a single word or small phrase, to describe the state of the union. While different people used different words, the meaning throughout these conversations was unmistakable, and deeply sobering. Here are some of the words and phrases that we heard: *screwed, Titanic 11, corruption, dysfunctional, failure, manipulated, deceived, a rude awakening, barely treading water*. These words and phrases describe a common condition: they reflect an inability to see and hear one another, to speak to common concerns, to get things done *together*. They reflect a lack of belief in something larger than ourselves. These are words and phrases people use to describe their lives in the Tower of Babel.

Sadly, in this environment there is little room for people and their concerns. A sense of humanity has been temporarily stripped away. And the building blocks people need to reach to pursue their aspirations have crumpled. The very conditions that enable people to make their lives whole and hopeful have gone missing. If there is a crisis in the nation, then it is in the very foundation that is required to create the kind of communities, the *society* that people want. This foundation is dangerously in peril. It must be rebuilt.

People are, thankfully, not utterly without hope. Over and over again in these conversations participants would affirm what has been the enduring power of America and her people. A Jacksonville woman put it this way: "When things are at their worst, we are at our best." Still, people say that to move ahead they must restore their faith in themselves, in one another, and in the country itself. A New York City man said simply, "Well, we certainly need to raise the faith in America. That's for sure."

> *It is clear from the people we met across the country that the challenges we face are more fundamental, more human, and much more provocative.*

Thus, the sample of Americans we met do believe in this country; but the nation has undergone—and *continues* to undergo—significant changes. People are in search of responses that acknowledge these changes. They are ready to come together and roll up their sleeves to address new realities. But this will happen only under the right conditions. As a Dallas woman put it, "I think this is still the land of opportunity. It's not the world as we knew it, but we're going to have to be more creative in building a new world." And a Detroit woman remarked, "I wouldn't want to live anywhere but here; but I think now we've just gotten to a point that *now* something needs to be done."

For now, then, the Tower of Babel and its noise dominates the landscape. At times the noise can be deafening; the path forward is not always clear. As one Champaign man said, "Just like if you're in an auditorium. If you go to a symphony hall and you hear the noise but you can't key in on what people are saying. You hear all of this noise if you go to a stadium, but you cannot particularly hear exactly what's being said." A woman, a fellow Champaign discussion participant, added:

> There's too much noise. Those that are making the decisions for the country have left the table. This one is standing on his soapbox yelling this, and then one is going off to chase Sally Sue, and everyone has their own agenda. So then the little people are being hurt by the decisions that they make; we're just being muffled out.

What happens when such noise comes to overwhelm people's lives, when there seems to be little opening for moving forward, when people feel they and the country are stuck or stymied? A Sonoma woman said that some significant disruption in the current order of things would need to take place for people and the country to find a new course. "It's going to take something really major in order for us to come together," she said.

To find a way forward we must understand where we are; only then can we discover a new path—and perhaps learn how to move beyond this Tower of Babel!

But to find a way forward we must understand where we are; only then can we discover a new path—and perhaps learn how to move beyond this Tower of Babel!

3

OUR INNATE POTENTIAL

One way out of the Tower of Babel is to take claim of what is good and right in the country and build from there. We must tap into the innate goodness and potential within each individual to counter the negative conditions overtaking the country. The reality is that this potential already resides within each of us; it reflects enduring values and beliefs people have long cherished. Sometimes the most vital solutions are closest to us, if only we open our eyes to them.

Sometimes the most vital solutions are closest to us, if only we open our eyes to them.

This truth the discussion participants discovered themselves. Over a number of hours they talked about the condition of the nation, the state of politics and public life, the chief concerns in their own daily lives. Time and again they returned to outline a constellation of values and beliefs they say have been temporarily lost in society, perhaps misplaced, shunted aside at times. According to these participants, these values must be reasserted if people are to create the kind of public discourse, interactions, and pathways forward that they want.

We identified the most prominent of these basic values earlier. One is compassion—the need for people once again to see and hear each other, reach out to the other, and support one another. Another is the importance of children—viewed as a gauge of the very health of our society and the basis upon which to build the future. Another is openness and humility together—which means room to engage with others, listening attentively, to discern what's truly important and to act with care. The last value in this group is concern for the common good—to believe we hold *shared* interests, at a time when people are implored daily to think essentially about their own survival, their own good.

Together, these values reflect a deep desire among people to reclaim a sense of humanity in society, and in their daily lives.

Together, these values reflect a deep desire among people to reclaim a sense of humanity in society, and in their daily lives. They are rooted in the belief that no one can go it alone at this time; and that, fundamentally, people and human interactions are the lubricant to make our lives, and the nation, work.

Of course, these values alone could never replace the need for strong and relevant programs, initiatives, and policies that may be required to address pressing issues. But without these values—without this human dimension—we lose the ability to guide the country in ways that reflect the best parts—or at least the better parts—of us all.

It's essential not to mistake people's desire to embrace such enduring values as merely a nostalgic plea to herald again some past era. It is not a knee-jerk attempt to hide one's head in the sand and disregard what's happening in the world, only to wish for imagined "better" times. Rather, it is about the rediscovery of fundamental, everyday behaviors that must be reclaimed and rekindled in our individual and collective lives, but adapted and put into action for these times, *our* times. It is the belief that what needs to be done is basic and close to home—and that many of the answers we seek are alive within us. It is about tapping into people's own capacity to step forward and exercise their innate power.

In this chapter, I offer a sampling of the language that the discussion participants used in speaking or alluding to these values.

COMPASSION

In Detroit, after much conversation, the moderator asked:

"What gives you hope?"

A man answered, "A more compassionate society."

"Compassion?" the moderator asked.

"Compassion, listening," the man replied.

What does it mean to be compassionate and for compassion to engender a sense of hope among people? The answer, is that more people must be willing to step forward and be in relationship with others—to see and hear one another, to acknowledge each other's pain and aspirations, to know that we cannot go it alone in life. Then compassion can be a guiding force for the nation and produce the hope people yearn for.

This call for compassion, and its vital importance in our collective lives, could be heard in each and every discussion group that we encountered. Here is one exchange between two participants from Detroit in response to a question about how compassion might play out in daily life. A woman said that compassion starts with an individual's "honesty and perseverance." Then she added: "You just need to push for what you want these days, and you need to be a good person. You need to do unto others as you would want to be done to you." A man spoke up: "Do unto others as you would have them do unto you. That's really good words, I believe, to live by, I mean, The Golden Rule."

By definition, "The Golden Rule" requires more than a single individual taking action alone. It involves oneself *and* others. A *relationship* is involved. But for many discussion participants, The Golden Rule has nowadays taken a back seat to other pressing matters in their lives, such as getting ahead or, more recently, making ends meet. But the message in this group was, that in order for the country to change course, compassion must be firmly at the center of our individual and collective lives. As one Denver woman put it, "I do a lot, and I just feel that sometimes … we're so busy in our own lives." Then, in reference to people making room to express compassion, she said, "But you've got to make that step, you've got to take that step, whatever it might be."

In Dallas, a mom explained how she hopes to hand down an ethic of compassion within her family.

One of the things I made [my daughter] do, one year,
for Thanksgiving was that she had to go serve at the food
kitchen—and so she learned that it wasn't all about *her*. You

know, there were people out there that have needs beyond what she sees on a daily basis. And I'm hoping she's going to do the same thing with my grandson.

At least a handful of people in each group would tell of their own personal experiences working in a soup kitchen or taking their kids to serve food to the homeless on holidays. Each story seemed to contain a moral lesson about how they wanted to conduct themselves in the world. These stories were like small proof points, personal reminders, about people's innate capacity to be compassionate.

At their core, these conversations about compassion turned on people's sense of humanity—and their worries

People must be willing to step forward and be in relationship with others—to see and hear one another, to acknowledge each other's pain and aspirations, to know that we cannot go it alone in life.

that somehow we have lost sight of *people* in recent times, replacing human relationships with consumer products, getting ahead, and gridlocked politics. Now, they say, we must return to the most basic elements of living in the world together.

One Jacksonville woman said compassion is about the "human condition," and went on to say, "I think that's just part of us, the human condition.… When, if someone falls, you run and pick them up." A fellow Jacksonville woman explained the importance of cultivating a compassionate impulse within and among people and what it would take: "How do you get there? … It starts with each and every one of us doing what we're supposed to do, and doing something for somebody else."

Note the phrases people used when talking about compassion—*human condition*, *The Golden Rule*, *honesty*, and *perseverance*. And notice, too, that their desire is not about getting credit or gaining recognition for their compassionate acts. In fact, just the opposite is true. As a Bend woman said, "The importance of giving, and giving without getting acknowledgement or recognition for it, is the biggest, most rewarding thing you could ever do." A Baltimore woman expressed a variation of this thought: "People are born compassionate. Being un-compassionate is a learned behavior."

CHILDREN AND FAMILY

In my own work with communities, when I hear adults talk about issues involving children and families, oftentimes they sound as if they are pining for their own childhoods and a return to "back in the day" when things seemed less complicated and easier. But this was not the case in these conversations. Listening closely to what people had to say, one hears something more provocative than a simple reflexive desire to recapture the past. People hold deep fears about the plight of children and worry whether young Americans are receiving the necessary guidance to become self-supporting adults and good citizens. This discussion, then, was at once about the future of individual children and the health of our communities. In people's minds, these factors are inextricably linked.

Here's how this perspective played out in a New York City conversation: "You don't see as many kids out playing on their bikes," a woman said, "or playing on the sidewalk as you would have 10 years ago." Note that her reference point is a mere "10 years ago," already part of this new, young century, and not from her own childhood decades earlier. Another woman built on the comment: "I agree. I have three children and I say all the time, 'You've got to go outside.' I mean, they never ask to go outside. All they want to do is sit in the house on Facebook or with the little cell phones and things like that…. This generation of children, they're all technical." Then, a third woman brought in a larger point about the community: "That also adds to the lack of communications skills in children, and that leads to the lack of community." This last concern was a theme throughout the conversations. As one Denver woman put it, "[Technology] is teaching our children not to be social. They don't have any social skills. They're very rude!"

The conversations about family and children revolved again and again around values of connectedness, perseverance, The Golden Rule, hard work, and love. Again, these values are seen as part of the counterforce to current negative conditions in people's lives and in the country. In this regard, one Dallas woman, echoing many group participants, expressed concern about too many children having to go it alone in their lives. "Some parents leave their children to raise themselves. We see it in education all the time." But the challenge involves even more than that, she pointed out: "There are some families that are just so stressed, they're doing everything they can, and the kids have to get their information from outside the home or be left to their own devices. Hopefully they've had instilled in them [somewhere] that they need some values and some commitment to being a good person." And a Baltimore man asked: "What about the emotional wellbeing of our kids? There are so many fatherless homes. Kids are growing up without dads, and I think that's a clear sign that things aren't really good. What's happening to these kids without dads?"

These conversations prompted many discussion participants to reflect on their aspirations for raising their own children and the day-to-day difficulties in making a good go of it. Here's a Champaign woman: "You try to teach your children that a measure of a man is not by what he has, but by whom he influences and how he spreads his legacy, more than anything. For me, that's how I want my children to grow up. I want my children to treat people the way they want to be treated. I want common courtesy, common decency." She continued, sadly, "And there's not that." Here, this woman may be reflecting as much on her own children as on the children of others.

The gap between what people see every day and what they want for children was a recurring concern. "You want to teach them to be honest," said a Detroit woman. "I have a six-year-old. I just pray that he grows up to be successful and honest and caring."

At the heart of moving ahead productively is clearly the need to cultivate values like honesty and caring within children; but even that alone will not be enough. Children must learn what it means to live out those values in the face of adversity. They must have the resiliency to bounce back in the face of setbacks. And they must be prepared to create a good and right course for themselves, over time.

To learn how to apply good values in everyday life came up when group participants talked about recent moves in education and youth sports, among other places in society, to build kids' self-esteem. Here's how one Jacksonville man put it: "Well, those who have been in education, or those who are recipients of education as well, there was a big push on self esteem." He continued, "It was almost to the point of being artificial. You would praise a student for doing his homework!"

Now, with the word *artificial*, this Jacksonville man had put his finger on an underlying rub at work throughout all the discussions about why, among so many issues, "getting back to basics" becomes so vitally important to people. As you will read in these pages, it is the *artificial* that people want to move to repudiate. It is the authentic that they seek. They have had enough of make-believe environments and discussions that seem to marginalize—even sometimes make non-existent—things that matter most to them in their lives. It is this very *distortion* of reality that drives people away from one another and from the public square. "Back to basics" is for them about focusing on what is real in people's lives; it is to stay grounded in what is important.

Absent this grounding, people question the purpose of their engagement and its value. They feel untethered from things that give meaning to their lives and to the lives of their children. They worry that they have rendered up control of what matters most to them. And this is a recipe for lost hope! It is a forced return to the Tower of Babel—where the keys to the exit doors have been thrown away!

Much to their chagrin many people said that on many youth sports teams every kid now receives a trophy, regardless of whether the child's team was successful—another artificial reward. The sense among discussion participants was that too much emphasis has been placed on making kids *feel* good—rather than helping them to *do* good, especially when the right thing can be difficult to do. A Dallas man put it this way:

Young kids, they're coming up, and they don't understand. When they run into a problem in a particular subject, they get flustered so fast and so easy. "Oh, I don't—I can't get it within five seconds." I'm sorry. I'm just not receptive to it anymore. And I'm like, "No, you just have to keep trying hard on this." This is—it's a life lesson that a lot of kids today don't really know anymore.

And another Dallas man said, "A lot of people don't understand that in order to be successful, you've got to put in a lot of work.... Kids are growing up not really understanding the value of the dollar nor understanding the value of hard work."

Instilling stronger values in children comes back to the role of adults and the community-at-large. "That's why you need parents that are leading the kids," asserted a Jacksonville woman, "because if you're only watching the tube ... if your kids are only doing that, they're not going to be led in the right direction." A Nashville man said that it was the responsibility of parents and adults to make sure this happens. "As individuals, we need to teach our children responsibility." And a Champaign man warned that money alone cannot address these concerns, that adults must step forward and show kids they care:

> At the end of the day, a lot of kids are leaving home, going to school without father figures in their lives, without people that actually show that they care. It's easy to go in your pocket and throw a few dollars. But, when you're talking about kids that are actually looking for love in all the wrong places, when they can see that adults have come together and are in the position to share what their own personal experience is ... what we may look at as someone being a volunteer could be that same person that impacts a young kid's life and actually puts them in the direction that makes them become more vision oriented.

SIMPLER LIVING

The conversation implying our need to go back to basics emerged in part from people's growing and frustrating realization about their own desire to always *want more*—the bigger home, more toys for their children, a boat, and higher incomes, among other wants. But these desires have taken their toll, people now say. People have heard a wake-up call. As one New York man said, "We're all asking, 'How much is enough?'" Another New York participant observed, "We can't take things for granted." Over and over we heard people say that they—*we*—have come to expect too much. A Champaign woman was more specific: "We're all striving for sort of the wrong things today in American culture. We want to be able to say we have the 7,000-square-foot house and the 6 bedrooms and 8 bathrooms and things like that. What's it for? Why do you need it? What is that about?"

> *People have heard a wake-up call: "We can't take things for granted."*

Another New York man summed up what many were struggling with, when he said: "I'm trying to figure out how much is enough? I mean, we're a very consumer-based country. When do we get to a point where we start to pull back and maybe use this as a healthy renaissance, and say, 'Enough is enough with all this stuff! How much do I need in my house? How much money do I need to spend?'"

This push for simpler living has been a topic in the United States and throughout the world for some years now. And many people's recent quest for a simpler way no doubt is a product of a new economic reality taking hold in the country, which has upended many people's lives and led many people to believe they must now build a life that is more manageable, more realistic, and more sustainable. A Sonoma woman observed this change in herself, saying there had been "A huge shift in me about how I look at things and what I buy and how much stuff I have. I'm not going down that path anymore. I think it was fueled by the economy and that everybody should own a home and all that other stuff. Why not me, and grab the brass ring? But I think at least in the people that I associate with, we've all changed that aspect; I definitely think it can be done. It's not all hopeless. There's hope. There's change." And then there was a Bend woman who talked about the growing pains associated with this shift:

> I feel like we're having a shift in mentality and in perspective, and I think it was much needed for this country. You don't have to keep up with the Joneses—you don't have to have these big, excessive houses and beautiful cars just to look good. And just to have this persona about you that you can't afford.… So this shift in mentality, I feel like our country is going through growing pains, and it's definitely rough. It's definitely rough when you go through a shift of this magnitude. But there's good learning. I honestly don't know how we're going to get out on the other side of it; but I ultimately think it is good. Hopefully it's going to turn around. It's like just make do with what you have.

What has changed in recent years is the extent to which this conversation is now more out in the open, where people want to engage fully with it. Here's how another Bend woman put it: "I think people are getting more used to a simpler way of living. I know we are." In talking about the adjustments her family has had to make in recent times, she brought the conversation back to *values*. She made this observation: "We look back and think we had the RV and the big home." Then, reflecting on the choices her family had to make, and what it means to raise one's children in this environment, she said, "My kids are 11 and 14, and I think it's been a good lesson for them to go through this and see their parents handle things tactfully and responsibly. I think this will be a blessing for their goals, to know how to handle their financial responsibilities responsibly." A New York City man told us about how he and his wife had decided to finally make a shift in their lives. "My wife and I are moving to a less dense area of the country because there [are] more resources, at least per person there." He continued, "It seems like it's so gloomy out in the rest of America."

For many, the American Dream—the one in which people expect to leave their kids with a better life than their own—now lies in tatters. People still want to fulfill that dream, but to keep it intact will require settling on a revised meaning to it. "America was built on, 'I want my kids to live better than I did—and their kids better than them.' That is the whole purpose of how the system was originally designed," said a Sonoma man. "[But] people need to learn moderation. Just because you have 30 credit cards and charge everything does not mean you *need* 30 credit cards and you can *charge* everything." And a Denver man said, "I think it's a good thing we're being forced to get by with less."

For at least some people this desire for a simpler life happened long before the current "Great Recession" hit. But, as one Bend man pointed out, better late than never, for those who hadn't made the switch yet.

Personally, I don't think I ever would have needed a bad economy, a turn for the worse, for me to start appreciating my family, the things that are important to me in my life. That's something that should have been—that you were raised with, that was nurtured when you were younger about appreciating what you have, as opposed to, "Oh, the economy's really bad. Oh, look how so-and-so's reacting to all this." Well, that's probably a good thing. That should have been already happening.

But for many people, the truth is, these difficult times have been an unexpected jolt. "Enough is enough!" they've said. They are looking to make adjustments in their lives, to live in simpler ways, where they are more grateful for what they already have.

OPENNESS AND HUMILITY

Discussion participants say too much *certitude, obfuscation*, and *false heroism* have overtaken and distorted people's interactions, public

Without more openness and a sense of humility, the roads to a better future are closed.

discourse, and the ability to move ahead together. This is what the Tower of Babel has brought on. What's left is a dangerous crowding out of people's reality and a sense of possibility about the future. Without more openness and a sense of humility, the roads to a better future are closed.

Part of this challenge is that people seem to gravitate to information and perspectives that serve only to confirm their own preconceived views, something that many academics and other analysts have researched and explored. This approach to life in America frustrated many people in our discussions. One Champaign woman said that she pined to understand different points of view:

I just wonder what's so threatening about information
and what's the impact on the political system? If more
conservative people than me, or more liberal people than
me, have a bias, I want to understand that bias. I think as a
society, we're losing our objectivity of really questioning.

People in these groups kept returning to our individual and
collective inability to question, to be open, to weigh different perspectives. One Detroit man expressed deep frustration that so many
public conversations have been held hostage by those who insist that
their point of view must rule the day, seemingly without regard to
find ways to get things done. He complained, "It's just either your
way or your way!" He continued, "What about someone else's way?
I mean, let's get something done!"

A New York City man wondered why it was possible some years
ago to bridge divides but not today.

I've seen the differences, I've seen the effects, and it's gotten
worse and worse over recent years. I really don't know the
answer to the question of why. If you want to go back to the
1980s, there were as strong opinions on both sides of the
aisle between people who were Reagan partisans and people
who were on the side of Tip O'Neill. But still there was the
ability for those people to get together and do something
for the interests of the country, even if neither side would be
totally happy with whatever got done. Why have we reached
the point where that seemingly cannot happen?

For the Americans we met, too many decisions are being made
without the benefit of exploring more options, more ideas. They

know that progress cannot come simply by remaining locked into rigid, unwavering, pre-set solutions. Furthermore, people say a fear of failure has grown among leaders, and perhaps in the rest of country too, crippling efforts to put the nation and people's lives on a different course.

And yet one of the first lessons in creating change—any kind of change, whether in one's personal life or in the life of a country—is exactly that an unwillingness to seek out a broad range of ideas, coupled with the fear of failure, is a sure-fire way to stifle needed creativity and innovation. The call here is for leaders *and* everyday people to embrace a set of straightforward *values* to help counterbalance these politically toxic, acrimonious, and close-minded times. People believe it is time to have an open mind and walk more humbly.

Thus the day of the heroic leader who professes to have all the answers—or in some omnipotent way to know the way forward—is over. People want to turn their collective attention to working out problems rather than endure more empty rhetoric and unfulfilled promises. A Las Vegas man, speaking about what he would say to leaders in this regard, put it this way, "You're not standing on a mountain preaching. All right? You guys are American citizens, each one of you. Sit down, have a civil conversation." Then, when he continued, he gave voice to a desire many discussion participants expressed: "Both sides have points that they want addressed. You can talk about them. That doesn't cost you anything." And he might have added: its value is priceless.

A Champaign woman told us, "I think there are too many people trying to be head honchos." And a Dallas man who said that the days of relying on celebrities and the like for leadership will no longer do. What was needed now, he said, was "stronger leaders, someone to follow. We need to put this out as the new standard—not a ball player, not a criminal, not just an entertainer—but someone who does good for their neighborhood, for their surroundings."

A Champaign woman articulated what many participants seemed to be searching to say: "I'm not looking for perfection. I'm looking for consistency." And listen to a Jacksonville woman who said about leaders, "I need you to do what you said you were going to do" —only to add, "And if you have to, you know, take a detour, bring me up to speed." Of course, doing the latter demands a healthy dose of humility: to acknowledge that a previous set of actions had not worked as anticipated, that a new direction was needed, and openly to come clean and tell others about it—*this* would require people to stop turning so quickly, and reflexively, on others, oftentimes seeking to place blame at others' feet when things have gone wrong. As one Las Vegas woman said, there is the impulse to "want to save face" by blaming someone else. She continued, "If they seriously care about the country, and have the country at heart, and what's best for the people, then they need to sit down like adults and quit going over this airway and that airway. Just sit together and work it out.… It's ridiculous." Here, openness and humility, what the woman was calling for instead of the many dodges of saving face, is a powerful antidote.

Finally, a woman from Bend offered this test to *anyone* who seeks to lead: "I think if you feel you're in a place to lead, you need to think about *can* you lead and have integrity? I think it's really important, because I think that's why we're feeling disenchanted about our current situation. People have not followed through having values and ethics. And those are really important things."

COMMON GOOD

When previous Harwood studies would ask people about the common good, they sometimes might sit in silence or confusion. The phrase—*common good*—seemed too abstract to many, outside their daily lives. But not this time; here, people leaned forward in their chairs and wanted to talk.

After long discussions about the state of the union and people's lives, we would ask what, if anything, the "common good" meant to people. A Jacksonville woman captured what many people expressed in these groups. When it comes to the common good, she said, one has to "give a little to get a little." She went on to explain: "Not meaning, where I'll give you this, if you give me 50,000 of that. I mean for the better good of the people."

A Sonoma man asserted that the common good is about taking actions that benefit the larger society rather than a single person, group, or business:

> You live by a set of rules that everybody should play by so that it provides the most benefit for the most people. Like, for instance, taxes. I mean, when you look at taxes, why is it that GE pays less taxes than I do? That's not the common good. That's "GE's good." But they have the money to put into people and power and to keep it that way. That's not the common good. That's GE's good.

Perhaps most piercing of all was the continued restatement that runs throughout so much of these conversations: we must "realize we're all human." As one Jacksonville man put it:

> Tragedy makes us realize we're human, even politicians; we dehumanize them. Sometimes when we see tragedy, we realize,

"Hey, this isn't a politician, athlete, a thirdworld country, or whatever. This is just a person in need, and they need us." That's when I think we all realize, okay, let's go ahead and do something.

Many daily tendencies and behaviors have taken us away from this simple but obviously critical guiding insight. The common good is about embracing *new* rules that work for the *greater* good rooted in people's lives, their aspirations, and their concerns. In this way, the common good is about crossing existing fault lines, boundaries, and walls that all-too-often prevent people from coming together. "I think there's such a thing as the common good, something that everybody can benefit from, regardless of status, Democrat, Republican, rich, poor, middle class," said a Detroit man. "I think there *is* such a thing."

> *The common good is about crossing existing fault lines, boundaries, and walls that all-too-often prevent people from coming together.*

But exactly where does the common good emerge from, especially in a society so riddled by acrimony, divisiveness, and isolation? Many in these discussions talked again about values already within people waiting to be tapped. "I personally believe that everyone has the common good on the inside of them," said a Champaign man. "However, often, people get so consumed in their 24 hours that they become out of touch with what we really need to happen." Again, the very values we cherish most can be shunted aside by the unexamined activities of our crowded daily lives.

At times, however, in people's lives, there are little reminders about the potential for common good, or at least a foundation upon which it could be built. Here's how one Las Vegas man put it:

With people, yes, there is a common good. Neighbors are out there helping each other. You live in your neighborhood and you're working on your car, one of your neighbors is a mechanic, he comes down and gives you a hand. You're in a grocery store line and someone's 50 cents short, and you reach in your pocket and give the cashier 50 cents. The people, there is a common good. As Americans and people, we want to see each other succeed and help each other.

A Bend man and others in his group viewed the public library in their town in this way. "You know, I think of our public library—if anybody goes to the library in Bend, I mean—I'm amazed at how it's a-bustle. It's a hustle and bustle [of] activity going on, and it's just amazing. If there's something that represents the common good, I would say it's the Bend Public Library." His comments echo those described elsewhere in this book—about the need for common space in which people can come together, in community.

Finding the common good is much the same process as making a real part of everyday life the other values highlighted by the discussion participants in this book: it becomes possible only when people are in relationship with one another, if they are willing to look to the other. It is possible only when people are willing to *engage* together. Take, for example, how this Jacksonville woman sees the task of exercising the common good:

You have to be able to exercise the common good, but you also have to be able to see that in other people. You know, sometimes people are a victim of their circumstances, so they are unable to visualize that common good within themselves, and you are presented with the opportunity to extract that

from them. You say, "Hey, you have this going for you.…"
Then maybe that, you know, switches them around.

When participants talked about activating the common good
in themselves and others, they didn't shy away from the obstacles to
doing so. Said one Champaign man:

> It seems to me, as a people, it's easy to care passionately about
> your family, a little but more about your neighbors, about the
> community. The question is how far can we extend the reach
> of our sympathy, our understanding, and our concern? Can
> we care enough to do something that is of value to the whole
> country? Can we care enough to say we are the citizenry, and
> *we can*? It seems to me that is what has vanished somewhat in
> recent times. We no longer have that sense of commitment.

Such a commitment will include the recognition of some basic aspects of ourselves and in each other. Listen to where a Dallas
woman took her view of the common good: "The common good is
making sure that everyone in society has an opportunity—to make
sure that we're all taken care of." Then, she added, "We all want the
same things, ultimately."

4

THE ABYSS

There always are twists and turns in any story, and this one is no different. As the previous chapter outlined, one clear path out of the Tower of Babel is for people and the nation to focus on re-igniting cherished values in our daily lives, including those of compassion, the importance of children, openness and humility, and concern for the common good. This will require that each of us step forward and tap our own innate power and potential to help the country and ourselves get back to basics. This is an essential step. Unfortunately, it may not be enough. For as people engaged in these discussions, something more troubling emerged and took shape: a complex set of challenges in which, people say, they and the country now are dangerously entangled.

Part of this sense of things no doubt is a result of the Great Recession and the huge toll it has taken on people; some of that tumult and impact is recounted in the pages that have preceded this and those that follow. But it must already be clear that people's concerns involve more than the economy—much more. Looming larger in their lives are longer term, insidious challenges that, now crystallized, are finally front-and-center. And they preoccupy America today.

Three such challenges were made clear in our conversations:

- People damning themselves for enabling a triumph of consumerism that envelopes their lives, drives their daily behaviors, and undermines the common good;

- Rampant mistrust of leaders, organizations, and even family members, which leaves people feeling empty, at loose ends, alone;

- Rigged rules in favor of the wealthy and powerful that make people believe the American Dream may be beyond their reach, leaving them with the feeling that they are left with little recourse.

Now, none of these challenges is new. They've been discussed thoroughly in popular and academic circles for years. What has fundamentally changed is this: these challenges have crystallized in

What has fundamentally changed is this: these challenges have crystallized in people's lives; they dog people daily; they have become inescapable, often inexplicable.

people's lives; they dog people daily; they have become inescapable, often inexplicable. And at times people feel little or no control over their lives, and far less able to affect the future. As one Denver man put it, "It feels like you're trying to walk up the down escalator sometimes."

Challenges that seem to have no resolution can produce potent emotions in individuals and the body politic. For one thing, they made people in our discussion groups dismayed: the challenges they identify have persisted over time, in fact worsened. And the long list of so-called "solutions" put forth to remedy them have generated big expectations but only limited positive impact. What's more, people feel a sense of deep personal remorse that they have played a role in enabling these challenges to take root and spread, and their own actions have failed to alter their course.

What's next on the horizon would seem to be the potential for more anger, more remorse—more pronounced and more paralyzing. But it is clear that more noise and recriminations, the pandering and selling of milk-toast solutions, will no longer work. People already know the score and believe the time for pretending is over. So, beware: this dangerous cocktail of anger and remorse will only grow, becoming more corrosive if the response to the challenges is not authentic, is not reflective of people's daily lives, and is not rooted in something real that people know and can believe. But for now, say the discussion participants, what is at issue is our *understanding* of the challenges. Will we acknowledge them? Will we turn away or toward them? Will we engage them?

People say we no longer have a choice.

TRIUMPH OF CONSUMERISM

This part of the story starts with a rampant consumerism and its ugly triumph. Over the years, I've written numerous studies that have discussed people's growing sense that consumerism has been overtaking their lives; their own deep internal conflicts about letting this happen; and their ambivalence about the possibilities and trade-offs that may be required in reining in these conflicts. Do I want more, or not? How much is enough? What am I actually willing to give up?

I can testify that these latest conversations have a substantially different feel and focus from earlier ones. Today, instead of talking about a *struggle* over consumerism, people say *the fight is finished*: consumerism has won. And the price, perhaps oddly, had not been anticipated.

People define the problem of consumerism as an all-encompassing desire for "instant gratification." One Jacksonville man preceded his comments on instant gratification with a cautionary warning: "I'm going out on a limb, so whoever has a saw and wants to cut it off, you can proceed." Then he went onto say, succinctly, "I think we have a situation here where people want instant gratification. They want everything now. We're not going to save it for later. We want it now!"

A Champaign woman made a similar observation, "One of the problems that our society has is that we have entered the 'here and now' of instant gratification." To a Las Vegas woman, the result was an impulsive nation. "I think America is like a very impulsive society," she said. "When you hear that you can text right now, you're more likely to want something at that moment than wait for something to come."

A desire for instant gratification has led people to feel they've lost control over their lives and over the nation itself. A New York City man said: "The extremes of instant gratification that people of all financial levels experience now is just out of control, totally out of control." The result, he said, is that life has become all about "what we can do to ourselves, or for ourselves, immediately." As a Baltimore woman said, "What's in it for me!"

At the heart of this impulse to gather up more and more—and now!—plainly sits greed. Speaking about the nation's current conditions, a Champaign man observed, "I think one of the biggest problems is greed, you know. There's absolutely no denying that." Left unchecked, said one Detroit woman, people's appetite for more is insatiable. "Because, you know, the more you get, the more arrogant you get; the more greedy. You can never have too much."

People believe that they and others are spending money they do not have and that a sense of entitlement has taken hold in the country. One Jacksonville woman put it this way: "We all spend money that we don't have; and that I deserve something—that's

As desire for instant gratification has led people to feel they've lost control over their lives and over the nation itself.

the general mentality." To many, the current situation is confounding. As a New York City man put it, "It's not making any sense."

For some discussion participants, this sense of consumerism, of greed, and of the desire for instant gratification knows no boundaries and has seeped into all segments of society. As one New York City woman observed, "I think that a lot of people are living beyond their means; and not only just at our level here, but politicians and the government and everything. That's why we have such a high national deficit." A woman from Bend saw other implications: "We're not a long-term investment country at this point. Maybe we were in a generation way before me; but the generation that I live in right now—and the generations that are living now that are coming after me—there's just a lot of short-term stuff. It's pretty frightening."

When people were asked to sum up how they would characterize themselves and their fellow Americans, the results were damning, and included such words and phrases as, *spoiled*, *self-centered*, *sense of entitlement*, *selfish*, *ungrateful*, and *narcissistic*.

Just where does all this lead? On the current path, the future was clear to these discussion participants. Here is how a New York City woman saw it: "I feel like everyone's looking out for themselves; the Republicans, the Democrats, the corporations looking out for their shareholders. There's no shared vision. I think that's what we need."

IN NO ONE WE TRUST

Imagine sitting in a room and asking people a basic question about their lives—and there's nothing but silence. That's exactly what happened in each group discussion when the Americans we encountered were asked to name leaders they trust. "You can hear the crickets now," was how one New York City man described the silence. In each of the conversations, participants were told they could name any individual, at any level of society, in any part of American life, and in any position. Still, all one could hear was the silence.

Inevitably, in most groups, one or two individuals would eventually break the long silence and offer up the name of a single leader or two whom they trust. Among the smattering of names mentioned were President Obama, a local state senator, the Dali Lama, US Senator Carl Levin (MI), and General Colin Powell. But when it came to such names, for the most part, no two people in the same group mentioned the same person. And there was little overlap, if any, among people's responses across groups.

In previous Harwood studies, and in our various on-the-ground initiatives across the country, we have found that people in most communities could name individual leaders they trusted. In some communities—those with a particularly strong civic health—the lists were quite long. In more "down-and-out" communities, people might mention only a few leaders. But seldom was there a *total* absence of trust.

There was a void in the conversation when we asked about trustworthy leaders this past year, however. It was as if leaders have disappeared or become irrelevant. Perhaps they also had become, in some cases, more human. As one Sonoma woman put it, "Maybe we shouldn't depend on leaders so much. They are human just like the rest of us. We're all frail." A Champaign woman made this comment: "I think people are very unhappy, and they feel that they don't have a voice, and they're looking for a way to have their voice heard, have a representative."

So, then, whom do people trust, if anyone? After the stretch of silence, and then the few names that might emerge, someone would hesitantly ask, "Can I mention my pastor? Does that count?" Another participant would mention his or her dad or granny or husband or wife. In each group one person, often more, would identify "God." In some instances people talked about close relationships they had forged in their own personal lives, germane only to them; seldom, if ever, did they involve figures within public life or politics. These close relationships were something they could find ways to verify, for themselves, in their daily lives. A Nashville man said this: "I trust my wife and I trust my pastor. I trust me…. That's sad to say, but that's just kind of the world we live in now." One woman from Bend was even grimmer: "There isn't a single woman in the public eye that I would encourage my daughters to be like."

One discussion group was an exception—at least in one notable way. There weren't a lot of leaders the Detroit participants trusted. But there was one, where near unanimous agreement existed around the table. That person was OPRAH. And the reasons why became quite clear during the ensuing (and animated) conversation; and these reasons may be instructive to a broader conversation about leaders in our society.

People said that Oprah has proven to them that she understands their reality and the daily struggles they encounter. Despite her own wealth and fame, they feel she has walked in their shoes. Even more, they said, she has demonstrated a positive track record, over time, of sticking with issues that matter to people, returning to them over and over again. In these ways, they see Oprah as reliable, consistent, caring, and on their side. Furthermore, they said that Oprah routinely makes herself vulnerable—that she is real; she doesn't pretend to be above certain realities that all people must face, such as her struggle to maintain her weight, find love in her life, and make a difference in the lives of others.

People said that Oprah has proven to them that she understands their reality and the daily struggles they encounter. But, to ask the obvious, is Oprah enough?

Oprah meets one basic test of trust for people: "Don't just tell me what you think I want to hear. Show me." This is how a Nashville participant summed up trust

But, to ask the obvious, is Oprah enough? Surely, our communities and the nation will require more leaders than just a single individual from the world of entertainment—even if it is Oprah—to help move society forward. Yet sadly, a bare few such leaders were mentioned in these group discussions. In New York City, not a single person was named. After extended silence, one person said, "That sure says a lot—that we can't name one person."

When the conversations turned to the organizations and groups that people trust, the response was much the same as we encountered when asking about individual leaders: very few, if any, were named. When people did mention specific organizations, they often focused on large and established national groups, not local ones: Red Cross, March of Dimes, Physicians for Responsible Medicine, and NPR and PBS. People saw these few groups as reliable, consistent and, most important, working on behalf of people and communities.

Apparently people's lack of trust in anyone or any group now permeates their personal relationships as well. In 2005, the Harwood Institute prepared a study that became part of the book *Hope Unraveled: The People's Retreat and Our Way Back*, in which Americans were found to be retreating from the public square into close-knit circles of families and friends. Now the stories from our group participants tell us that those close-knit circles have been violated, too. A Baltimore woman shared this story:

> I don't want to give my own personal examples, but a best friend of mine lost her job and her husband; she had a child. I felt pity and invited her into my house. She ended up stealing two of my purses out of my closet because she felt so desperate. I would have fed her. I would have done anything. But to steal? I don't think she was that kind of person; I'd known her for so many years. But I think that she felt so desperate that she did that.

There were many such stories; they poured out of people. This story came from a Las Vegas woman, "I lent somebody some money with the promise that I'd have it back, because I really didn't have it to lend. That's been a year ago." She says she has heard "every excuse in the world" about why the loan hadn't been paid back yet. A Detroit woman would not have been surprised: "Everyone is only out for themselves. If people get into a bad spot, or a hard time in their life, they're going to do whatever it takes to make themselves better. It doesn't matter if they take from a family member." There were many references to untrustworthy family members. A Champaign woman said: "My sister may steal from me, but I know I can still trust her with something. But I couldn't trust her to be in my house forever; or trust her with my money. Because I'm sure she'll pinch off of me." A Detroit man said much the same: "I've been burned too many times by friends and too many times—I hate to say it—by family members, too. But my wife hasn't stabbed me in the back *yet*." Yet another such comment came from a Denver man who perhaps was lamenting the situation in his own family as well as in others he knows: "You can't even get immediate family—very rarely do you see immediate family support each other."

For a final comment, out of many, listen to the lack of trust that has come over a Jacksonville woman: "It used to be I would trust someone until they proved otherwise: they couldn't be trusted. However, through trial and error, I've been hurt by giving trust. That person did not come through. So now I am more distrusting. Sometimes I don't like to be that way, but it goes back to not wanting to be hurt."

Trust is the lubricant that enables society to function: for people to find ways to work together; for give-and-take to occur; and for progress to be made. Again, in this present study, we have found not so much a *lack* of trust in society, but an *absence* of trust. According to discussion participants, this absence of trust permeates people's lives—from the highest levels of elected leaders, to local leaders, to those individuals closest to us in our personal lives. Those we hold any real and abiding trust in are few in number.

So where does this overwhelming and pervasive absence of trust leave us? One woman from Detroit summed things up this way:

> I have taught my two [kids] to trust when it's deemed worthy to be trusted. If someone is feeding you a line, then you know it is what it is—because even though *you* may be trustworthy, there's a whole world out there that's not. And all of them have got pearly smiles, so you be careful of the wolf in sheep's clothing. This is what I teach them. You're going to have to hold your own. You have to hold your own. You have to be who *you* are regardless of who *they* are. So, if *you* want to be trustworthy, you have to know how to spot *them*. You're not going to catch them all, but you're going to have to know how to spot them, and that's just part of life.

For years, Americans have put their faith in the old adage: "If you play by the rules, anything is possible in America." But that notion—that *ideal*—is no more. This implicit social contract now seems like a relic of a bygone era.

RIGGED RULES

Many Americans argue that a whole set of rules has been rigged up against them, and they are at loose ends about how their lives will unfold and where the country is headed. This is a feeling that many discussion participants had. Of course, this isn't a new tension in American life or history. But what is especially noteworthy here is the extent to which people feel left behind and, accordingly, without any ability to exert control over their lives. For many, this is about how those with power win and those without power lose.

What's at play for people is a growing divide in a nation that is propelled by wealth, power, political connections, and access to

What's at play for people is a growing divide in a nation that is propelled by wealth, power, political connections, and access to opportunity.

opportunity. For many, this divide makes people feel that a basic sense of decency and respect for people is missing in our society. This sense that the deck is stacked against ordinary people, augmented by people's sense of loss, cannot be overstated. When people feel they have little control over their lives—when they believe they have no recourse—then cynicism sets in, and people feel bereft of possibility.

In Dallas, one woman talked about the divide simply and harshly: "Those at the top are getting paid, and those below are losing their jobs." In New York City, a man told the story of how his neighborhood had changed over recent years. When he bought his home, he paid $48,000, but now homes in his neighborhood are being sold for over $1 million. Here's a portion of what he had to say about how he sees what's happening:

> It's the wealthy people taking it over, and then they don't
> *live* there. It's vacant; or they rent it; or it's a vacation home;
> and this is a neighborhood for families. That's what it was
> intended for, but it's not. I mean, the rich are the powerful,
> and the powerful are the ones who make the rules.

Far across the country, in Bend, a woman told an eerily similar story about her neighborhood—about people hurting and others making gains at their expense. "It's becoming a neighborhood for wealthy people that are swooping up the deals now because people couldn't afford their houses. And now they're on short sales!" A fellow Bend participant talked about how this situation is only adding insult to injury, bemoaning, "The rich don't hire locals to do their work!"

This ever-growing divide is splintering the country. And the new rules that propel it are *remaking* the country in ways that are a far cry from people's aspirations, violating their sense of what America stands for. One Champaign woman spoke about the "haves" and the "have-nots":

> I think there's a real sort of disparity between the "haves" and the "have-nots." And I think the middle class is really kind of disappearing. I think a lot of families have been hit with unemployment and it's just becoming a harder and harder struggle to provide at all for your family. Then, at the same time, I think there's a group that is continuing to get wealthier and wealthier—and there's really a divide.

This divide, people tell us, is now being opened further, and exacerbated, by both the political "left" and "right" all for their own gain. This, in part, is what riles people so; the sense that they are being exploited for someone else's gain, while their concerns go unaddressed. They believe they have become pawns in a game that is unaccessible to them and shows little respect for them—or understanding of them.

The Champaign woman who spoke about the disappearance of the middle class lamented, "I think part of it is just the sense of that divide; that sense of sort of not understanding what the common experience is for residents of the country." When people find themselves under such immense stress and do not believe that anyone can hear their calls to mend breaches between their lives and the larger society, their lives may feel out of control, bereft of possibility. Worse yet, when those in power are the beneficiaries of change—and seem utterly oblivious to what's happening to others around them, many in need—people begin to conclude, as did a New York City man, "There are a lot of wealthy people who really have no clue."

This sense that rules have been rigged by those with power applies for the corporate world, too. Much has been written and reported in the popular news about outsized salaries for corporate chiefs, small corporate tax bills, banks and investment houses run amuck, and the like. Frustrations with such rigged rules—with a way of life gone seriously awry—deeply troubles people. Here's the view of a Denver woman: "When the housing market crashed we gave [lenders] money; then they gave it back. Meanwhile, they gave themselves millions of dollars of bonuses. You know, after we were in a crisis, they still gave themselves bonuses, and we accepted that. No one said anything about it." And in Dallas, a woman went right to the heart of the matter as many participants saw it, when she said, "I believe there is a lot of corporate greed and a lot of corporate opulence out there." And then there was the Bend woman, who said flat out, "Corporations are what run it all."

Listen to this Dallas man as he weaves together the threads about what's happening around him. Also take note of how he is not pining for some nostalgic past, but rather looking for answers about the future.

> I remember the way it used to be, where everyone helped each other; and now, unfortunately, companies are in business to make money. I know that, and I'm not going to discredit that. But they will let somebody go that's a better worker—because they're making a little more money—instead of somebody who can't get the job done—simply because they get to pay them less. And everybody I see out there—Walmart and everybody else—is providing less service, less product for the people.

What makes matters even worse, apparently, is that these group participants said leaders have adopted their own set of rules that inoculate them against the very pressures, realities, and fears that everyday Americans now face. This only fuels mistrust. One Detroit man said, "You know, the politicians: they retire, they get their pension, and they get all this stuff paid for until they die. I mean, why can't they take hits just like we do?" And here's a woman from Sonoma, "It's just obscene the way these people

When people feel they have little control over their lives—when they believe they have no recourse—then cynicism sets in, and people feel bereft of possibility.

are treated like kings and queens, like some kind of royalty. I feel like we're becoming the peasants." Another Sonoma woman offered this judgment: "They live good lives, they make good money. They're not struggling like the rest of us." And a Dallas man said, "Once a person gets into a political life, he's off into a different realm … [his]

own little black hole. And once they get up there, they forget about what we want or what we need." A Jacksonville woman remarked that, once elected, politicians believe they can act with immunity. "It's like they have authority to do whatever they want. They're above the law."

Ultimately people want to know "where is all this leading?" According to a Champaign woman, it's leading only to people feeling more desperation about their lives.

> I see one of the greatest reasons we have such a great divide
> is because of the politicians, because they have taken oil
> companies that made billions of dollars in profit; and, of
> course, these politicians are the ones who are lowering
> corporate taxes and raising taxes on those of us who make
> $30,000 or less. I mean that's—yes, they are contributing to
> the economic divide. They are contributing to, just basically,
> the desperation of the common person.

People say they have watched various wrong-doings brought to light as the rules in America have changed, with the Wall Street crisis being just one example. They also say that there have been no consequences. As one participant asserted, "No one has been convicted." Rigged rules leave people feeling there is no one or no place to which they may turn.

People in effect seem to be left facing the triumph of consumerism, unfettered greed, rigged rules, and the sense that they are on their own, their lives spinning out of their control.

5

A BROKEN MORAL
COMPASS

For people to move ahead from this view of life requires some modicum of hope; and hope comes from more than promises about change being on the way. It is a combination of faith in ourselves and in one another and a sense of possibility about the future. It demands reliable signs of progress over time. Each and all of these elements are dangerously in short supply. In fact, hope is not what people feel today, but rather a growing sense that things in their lives, and the nation, are coming ever-more undone. One New York City man put it this way: "We don't know what's going to come next." A Bend woman expressed her sense of things going bad by pointing to the many medications for depression and anxiety that television ads promote.

I think the country is really dysfunctional right now, like a chaotic family. It doesn't feel like there's a safe place anymore. We're not healthy. When I watch the news or a movie on TV, every other commercial is about a drug, a prescription drug for someone for anxiety, mental health, depression. "Here's a pill to help you."

Similar observations from participants in other groups all raise the same distressing concern, that, in effect, the nation is without a moral compass. One Jacksonville woman said, "In our society, we're taking a step back as far as small things, like family—our core values that we were brought up on.… I think now we're kind of straying away from them." Another woman responded, "I think our morality is at an all-time low. I don't know—I really haven't figured out— where it started going down, down, but I find it very sad." A Denver man also spoke in terms of morality saying, "Morality was more important to the older generation."

Then there is this story that came from a Detroit man:

My grandfather is a pastor, and we were driving, coming up the ramp on the freeway, where there was a guy standing with a sign, 'WILL WORK FOR FOOD.' So my grandfather said—now, he also owns an apartment building, so he said — "You know what? Why don't you come along with us? I have an apartment building and I have some work I need you to do." And so the guy says, "Well, that's nice, pastor, but if you're not going to give me at least $25 an hour, then I'm not going to go, because that's what I make standing right here on the corner just with the sign."

As this Detroit man recounted his story, people in his group shook their heads in dismay. They wondered how is it that things have come to this? Just where did we, as people, make the wrong turn? Listen to this Dallas woman, who sounds as if she had been sitting in the Detroit group miles away listening to the story about the pastor, his grandson, and the worker. She said, "I'm right there with you! I think we're getting really fricking lazy with everything—work, school…. You know, we're just like, 'Eh!'"

According to our discussion participants, much about our individual and collective moral compasses feels out of whack. A Bend man wondered, "How can we have a society where a baseball player makes $30 million a year and a teacher makes $30,000?" To him, and many others, such questions are rooted in a moral code that no longer reflects what people value,

> *According to our discussion participants, much about our individual and collective moral compasses feels out of whack.*

and no longer works for the country. Indeed, moving from a ballplayers to affairs of state, people see the same mistakes being made over and over, holding enormous implications for their future. Said one Champaign man:

> We've made an awful lot of bad decisions in the past. We didn't pay for the war in Iraq; we're not paying for the war in Afghanistan. That's limiting so much of our ability to respond in ways we need to, and it seems to me we're walking away from investment in our educational system. We're walking away from investing in people, and that's a disastrous consequence of bad decisions of the past. And the

extreme partisanship that animates the country now is just making it difficult to grapple with our problems; so we're *not* grappling with them.

Somewhere along the line, the individuals in these conversations believe, they and their fellow Americans have simply given up, or given in, to prevailing conditions and have been waiting—waiting for someone else to come along and fix everything. Said one Sonoma woman, "Americans, you know, for a long time, have been lulled into complacency." And here's how a Las Vegas woman explained this dynamic of waiting:

> People just get to the point like, okay, well, somebody else can handle it, or somebody else can do it. I've questioned a lot of things like, "Ooh, why is that?" Back in the day, people stood up and fought for what they believed in: they marched, they protested, they did all that stuff. But Americans now—we're just, "Okay, well, let somebody else handle it!"

Group participants used different words and ways to describe people's current state of mind. A Jacksonville man explained that too many Americans have become "spoiled," saying, "we need to work harder for things." A Las Vegas woman said the problem was laziness: "It's like a lazy mentality. It's like, okay, this needs to change, but then I don't want to do nothing to make it change."

Of course, change can be scary for people, especially those who are struggling just to hold on to what little they may have. Another Champaign man observed, "Well, I think people *are* afraid, and they're rightly afraid, because we have a system that creates sharper distinctions between winners and losers than it used to, and so this can cause people to behave … in ways to sort of maximize their chance of having success."

Sometimes the choices people face are excruciating. Listen to this story about a Las Vegas daughter and her mom, both of whom taught at the same local public school, and both of whom had to confront the harsh realities of today's world. The daughter told us, "I'm a teacher … me and my mother worked at the same school." When local budget cuts in schools were made, she said, "It was between me and her [in the classroom], so do you tell your mama to go or you go?" The daughter decided that she must leave. Now her mother sits in the classroom with 40 students, by herself, where learning has become much more difficult to pursue, and where classroom management has become the number one goal. Meanwhile, where is the daughter? At the time, she was unemployed and told us, "I must now go do something else, and I still have the student loans and everything else."

Pressure in people's lives is coming from all directions. "For people who are retired, you're sitting there watching your 401(k) go: there's another $50,000 gone and then another $50,000 gone, and so forth…. It is stressful because that's money that you've saved and you've lost, and you can lose it a great deal faster than you can recoup it," said a Jacksonville man. A Dallas woman told her group about a relative, whose painful plight was an all-too-common story in our conversations. "I have a relative living with me because he can't find a job in his field. He can't find anything but a very low-paying job, and he's been at the same profession for 30 years." A Baltimore woman spoke of people's hope just to survive: "I think everybody is trying to survive. People are trying to get through their day. Everybody's trying to make it in life—you work, you get home, you've got kids to take care of, and household things to do. Your days are just so busy." And then a Champaign woman reminded people that survival is different than greed. "I think people are more afraid of losing what they have. It's true you have those that are greedy. But then you have those that are just trying to hold on for the sake of their sanity to the little bit that they do have."

The changing circumstances of life today has led some people to wonder whether college is even the "right move" anymore, considering all the talk among experts and political leaders about people having to take advantage of post-secondary opportunities in order

Sometimes the choices people face are excruciating.

to make it in America these days. A man from Sonoma had a typical story: "I've got a friend who's working at a Mary's Pizza Shack, and he just graduated from college. He's like, 'I can't find a job.' It's sad, because you tell everybody that's the American dream: go to college, get a good job." A Detroit woman asserted, "It's hard for people graduating college to find jobs that pay enough money.… Graduating from a great school with a degree and still not being able to find a job—it's really hard. It's kind of scary." If college doesn't give people a leg up, they wonder, what will?

Oftentimes, as people recounted their personal experiences, others would whisper to someone sitting next them about how they had seen or experienced something similar. Others would simply give a knowing nod in responding to such stories. One New York City man said:

I think in America, with the affluent, what they're feeling is like a cold; but there are other people here in America who are catching pneumonia. I think that's the difference between the haves and the have-nots.… That separation unnerves me. It really does, because there are some people who are really, really, really struggling.

A woman from Detroit expressed a sense that things were spinning beyond her personal control. "I just feel there is a plot against people who don't have anything. People who have everything, they don't need help; but the middle class … we're just kind of losing it. I've lost a home. There are a lot of people who are losing their homes. What they're paying on jobs now, you need two incomes, and I'm widowed. I have to live with my sister-in-law in order to even make it."

One way to read people's concerns about the value of higher education—or about the many other challenges people have raised, for that matter—is simply as a reflection of the current difficulty of anyone finding a well-paying job. But perhaps people's comments are as much a reflection about the very unsettled "social contract" that has served for so long as a key reference point in American life. Over the years, that contract has offered people hope. But what if this social contrast is now … coming undone?

With the triumph of consumerism, rampant mistrust, rigged rules, and the like, people feel there is little for them to hold onto. Maintaining control in their lives has become increasingly difficult, at times out of reach. No matter that they recognize that they are partially to blame for these conditions. A Baltimore woman pointed out that there simply is a lack of clarity about what to do next. She said, "I don't think we're on a clear path, and I think it's very cloudy where we should go."

All this can lead people to take extraordinary steps in their lives, ones that perhaps they had never imagined taking before and that call into question their moral compass. One story in particular gives a vivid example of such behavior. It came from a 21-year-old Las Vegas male, who up to this point in the conversation had said very little.

He told us he works at a retail store in Las Vegas, and oftentimes when he looks out the store's big front windows onto the parking lot, he sees individuals waiting around until shoppers unload their shopping carts. After the customers drive off, he said he watched as these individuals went over to the empty carts, and then often plucked out a small piece of paper. He often wondered what they were doing and what they had found. Finally, one day, he figured it out. He could see these individuals, with the small pieces of paper in hand, come into the store. As he watched them, he saw them go to various aisles and pull products off the shelf. Then, they'd walk over to the customer service desk, and ask to return the product. As the group listened intently, he said he discovered that they were using the receipts from other shoppers to redeem products for cash. When he finished telling this story, almost as an afterthought, he said that the products people sought to redeem were not expensive ones, oftentimes for just $5 or $3.

So there are different dimensions to this loss of a moral compass. In some ways it is about people feeling so hurt and powerless that they are waiting for someone else to solve the pressing problems in society; in others, it reflects people feeling they must take their personal survival into their own hands, which might lead them down the path of those individuals in the Las Vegas parking lot, or to the actions of the individual who had refused the pastor's job offer, or the individuals mentioned in the previous chapter who apparently felt they must pilfer from their relatives. It also produces within and among people sheer anger about how some—such as bankers, politicians, corporations, and wealthy home-buyers, among others—have cooked up ways to benefit themselves despite, or maybe because of, the current state of affairs in the country.

A Dallas man explained that in these tumultuous times, people have "lost sight of what we actually need to figure out, so more of their energy is going to trying to make a good living than actually focusing on the next steps as a whole for the country." A Champaign man

"Where are we headed?"

added, "I think there are so many distractions that prevent you from being focused on what is the best thing to do. You just get so caught up." And a Denver main said, "The tougher it gets, the more you have to look out for yourself."

When we asked people in Bend to describe how after their long discussion these conditions left them feeling, three comments stand out. One participant said "Numb." Then another offered, "We feel so lost." And finally, a third person, giving voice to worry, said "Where are we headed?"

6

CHANGING TRAJECTORIES

Listen closely to people, and they will tell where we must head. What they want most of all is to find practical ways to get the country and their own lives pointed in a different direction. They want to set in motion a new and different dynamic that enables a move back to basics. And they seek to work through the entanglement of challenges they face. Importantly, all this must occur on a human scale—where people literally can create, and see, and drive this new trajectory; where the possibility to restore belief in themselves and in one another comes from taking action together. But what enables communities, a country, to move in this way?

Conventional wisdom would lead us down a well-worn path: (1) identify "the problem"; (2) send wise men and women off to engage in long planning processes; (3) emerge with yet another new, big, often "slick," initiative, program, or policy that promises to change the world—all of which serves only to deliver far too little and, ultimately, to dash people's fragile hopes. Business-as-usual will not make the cut for people—not this time.

The task, as people see it, is to kick-start a new trajectory where actions start small and local, between and among people; where clear goals are set and achieved, and where people can restore faith in themselves and one another and in the belief that Americans still can get things done *together*. Whatever these actions may be, they are not expected in themselves to solve our pressing needs. This is not their true or intended power. Rather, their intrinsic power is to signal to ourselves and others that we can undertake our common or shared business in more productive and promising ways. Through such forward movement people can rediscover and tap into their own innate power and potential to shape their environment. They can seize greater control over their lives and future.

Through forward movement people can rediscover and tap into their own innate power and potential to shape their environment.

People in these conversations are looking to press "reset"— yearning to take actions that are immediately valuable in their daily lives; and to start building a strong foundation that provides a platform for later efforts to come. As I have noted before, this does not mean that new or improved programs, initiatives, or policies are not needed; instead, the chief aim here is to provide a jolt to the system and gin-up a tangible counterforce that helps spark and leverage the change people are seeking by pushing "the system" from the outside, because incremental change from the inside has been elusive for so long. Absent this course, who knows what will happen? Probably more inaction; deepening mistrust; dashed hopes.

BECOMING A COMMUNITY

This part of our story, then, begins with a common resolution among people about what must happen in America if a new trajectory is to be successfully kick-started. We must dedicate ourselves to reweave our communities. This is an option that starts with people themselves. A Dallas woman said people can no longer wait for others to take action for them. "If the change is going to happen, it's going to be grass roots. We're going to have to spur that movement and keep it going." A Detroit woman echoed this sentiment, saying that only when people come together will there be any possibility to create the change they seek. People cannot wait for others, she said.

> I feel like we are not making our voices heard. You know, we can't expect [leaders] to just hear our voice and do it. We need to come together. There's a lot of us. There's more of us than there are the wealthy or companies, and if we actually went together and made sure our voices were heard, I feel like it would make a difference.

Yet we know from previous Harwood studies, along with studies from other individuals and organizations, that in recent times people have stepped away from the public square, retreating into small circles of family and friends (notwithstanding the brief excitement generated for many by the 2008 Obama campaign). Perhaps some people thought they could—even should—leave change up to somebody else. Recall the comment by the Las Vegas woman from the previous chapter:

> People just get to the point like, okay, well, somebody else can handle it, or somebody else can do it. I've questioned a lot of things like, "Ooh, why is that?" Back in the day, people stood up and fought for what they believed in: they marched, they protested, they did all that stuff. But Americans now—we're just, "Okay, well, let somebody else handle it!"

The problem now confronting people is that, amid all the changes enveloping the country and their lives, they find themselves feeling desperately alone, at times terrified they must "go it alone." In these conversations, the antidote is finding within themselves the courage to take practical steps forward and effect change *with others*. It is *in community* that people tell us they find numbers and strength to act.

But if people *were* to step forward, what then? Toward what purpose would they be guided? Is stepping forward simply about people coming out from their homes and doing something … anything? Are all actions of equal significance, of similar meaning? Not at all. In these times of fragmentation, isolation, and fear, people yearn for something more meaningful. They want a focus on actions that matter to them and to their communities—not simply to engage in make-work or blindly fall in line behind some organization so it can say it was able to mobilize a certain number of Americans.

During the Champaign conversation a man succinctly put his finger on what so many people in so many different ways, across all these varied conversations, had been expressing: "We really need to rebuild a sense of the civic community where people all are participating and various voices get heard in some kind of way so that that dialogue influences the decisions that are made. But this is not happening." The point is worth underscoring, because it is absolutely central to this

If a new trajectory is to be successfully kick-started, then we must dedicate ourselves to reweave our communities.

study. This gentleman, like many others in this study, believes that the essential task ahead is to *rebuild a sense of the civic community* and not get lost in mere activity. How and why people move forward counts.

START SMALL, START LOCAL

This notion of kick-starting things—by starting small and starting local—is intended to give the country a jump start, some juice so it can move in a new and better direction. People insist that the way forward is for them to take practical actions—rooted in their communities—that grow trust, building relationships and civic faith. This is what people desperately yearn for.

Before moving on, let's consider for a moment what this new trajectory is *not*, because getting this wrong would undermine what people are looking to do and leave them once again feeling alone, lost and anxious amid false hope.

- People do not merely want to launch thousands of little actions with no clear common purpose in mind.

- People are not calling for fast and easy actions—much like one hears oftentimes in the volunteer management sector nowadays—that seem geared more for an individual volunteer to have a personal experience than to create hope and change *in a community*.

- People do not have grandiose ideas about what they can accomplish together at the start. Nor are they looking for slick, highly packaged grand plans to mobilize Americans. They want real actions, rooted in realistic community expectations.

A Detroit woman brought out the significance of people's desire to start small, and local, when she said that when people engage in this way they "are becoming actively involved in what goes on in their community." She added, "They're getting to know people. They're getting to know what it's really like maybe to be an elderly person that's shut in; or to be, perhaps, a little kid that's got some major problems. Otherwise, we are just hearing about it, and we don't get involved. Involvement is really where the action is."

People insist that the way forward is for them to take practical actions—rooted in their communities—that grow trust, building relationships and civic faith. This is what people desperately yearn for.

Her point reminds us of people's desire to re-ignite a sense of compassion in their lives and in our larger society. For people to slow down long enough to realize we're all human. And her point reminds us about people's hope to return to the public square in order that they might take greater control over their lives and the direction of their communities. Indeed, the only way to achieve these goals is by being *a part of* the community. It is from these interactions—this *engagement*—that an authentic sense of possibility can arise.

This sense that change must start small, and local, and between and among people, emerged repeatedly, from one group to the next.

A Denver man underscored the need not to become too grand in one's view of getting started. "Maybe we're trying to think of huge world-changing things we could do versus joining your neighborhood cleanup." A Denver woman implored, "Just start small!" echoing the Nike tagline, "Just do it!" A Jacksonville woman gave a deeper sense of what becoming involved can mean:

> Think within where you live. I feel like I can make things better by, you know, volunteering in the school and being present for field trips and things like that. I think it makes a difference, because when I am there, I see the kids of the parents who are there and are involved. And the ones who aren't—and that gap is kind of widening, so I feel like that it does pay off, that it will benefit.

Her further comments reveal precisely why people want to start small *and* local. She pointed out that people want to forge genuine relationships with others; to know one another; to see for themselves what is actually possible in their community. In other words, people do not simply want to undertake activities for the sake of saying they are engaged, as if such activities are in and of themselves the end goal. Rather, they want to become engaged to see and hear one another and thus to rebuild trust.

RIPPLE EFFECTS

A story from Las Vegas helps to illuminate the essence of what it means to move forward by starting small and local, and building from there.

After some discussion, a man sitting near the middle of the table raised this idea: What about people painting a local neighborhood school together? The idea prompted people to start talking about how they could actually come together to make this happen. As they did, there was a palpable sense of excitement in the room, the sense of a possibility to move beyond the triumph of consumerism and misguided values in society.

The moderator, amid this excitement, began to press the group about whether painting a single school would really create the kind of change they were looking for in education and in society. People's response was quick and clear, and firm. They said that just painting one school could never address their larger aspirations and concerns. But, they continued, this small step was necessary to get things moving in a better direction. Kids would see that someone cares about them. A signal would be sent to other parents to get more involved in the school and in their children's education. The neighborhood itself might take greater ownership of the school and the rearing of children. But even these pay-offs, they said, were not what they had in mind when talking about painting the single school.

At this point, people in the group built off of one another's comments, oftentimes finishing one another's sentences. The pay-off, they argued, was that people in other parts of the community would see what was being done at this one school, and how people had come together, not to complain or argue, as they often do, but to create something together. When people came to see this, these Las Vegans said, it would demonstrate that things can get done, that people can work together, and that they can move forward. This would help people develop more confidence in their own abilities, the abilities of others, and of the community as a whole. Then things could keep building from there.

It is this chain reaction that people are in search of and believe must occur to kick-start and build a new trajectory. And they believe this is eminently possible. As another Las Vegas man put it:

> Basically, the more people [get out], the more sense of hope they'll get…. In their mind, they'll get out, they'll want to help, and when they see that they can get something accomplished together, they're going to be like, "Oh, we can get this accomplished. Let's get more people to work so we get something bigger accomplished. Let's keep on growing from that part on!"

It is taking actions close to home—with small groups of individuals—that enables people to take greater control over their lives as a community. And such actions serve to affirm what people already know in their hearts: that they must step forward with compassion, guided by a sense of the greater good. People say this new path—the forming, development, and, ultimately, the take-off of this new trajectory—will have an "infectious" quality in communities that will, as one Jacksonville woman put it, create the sense that "everybody can do something." She continued: "You know, one person can't do everything, but every single one of us can do something."

It is by doing—and by achieving things—that people grow excited about moving down a new path.

In none of these conversations did anyone offer, or say they expected, some grand scheme about how all these small steps would get started, take place, and grow. There was no suggestion that there would be—could be—some kind of big bang in which all of a sudden, in one fell swoop, *everyone* (or even many people at first) would become engaged and active. Rather, in the Champaign group, one woman told us that it would be impossible to think that 80 percent of people would automatically engage. But she did believe that 10 percent could, and then it could spread from there. Thus, she and others had a notion about how change might unfold over time: small actions, shining a light on them, giving others hope and confidence to step forward, then to keep moving forward. As she put it, "You can, you know, make a difference in small ways. And if that expanded, I think we could have a huge impact."

Pride plays a part in how these small steps can spread over time. A Las Vegas man, when asked about people stepping forward to get things done together, said: "I think people would take more of a sense of pride in this country, knowing that you're helping other people out, you're helping your community out. It would be a sense of pride."

But of course, none of this will happen without some form of leadership. Here, a Detroit man pointed out that one of the ripple effects when people start small and locally is "to lead by example, I mean, hopefully, somebody else will see you out there lending a helping hand." A Detroit woman said the chain reaction itself leads to the creation of new momentum. "If more people … are more hands on in the community, then it's going to eventually lead to better opportunities." Indeed, a New York City woman saw the benefits of this chain reaction as, "the trickle effect," how conditions come to change in a community as well as in the nation.

SETTING GOALS

The Las Vegas man who said that people would have more sense of pride by knowing they were helping others also said that when people find themselves involved in taking meaningful actions they'll discover their capacities grow: "Oh, we can get this accomplished. Let's get more people to work so we get something bigger accomplished. Let's keep on growing from that part on!" Setting doable goals, and achieving them, loomed large in people's thinking about how a new momentum will take hold, grow, and tap into people's sense of pride, leading to an ever-expanding constellation of actions.

It is by doing—and by achieving things—that people grow excited about moving down a new path. This is not a new theory, but simply a reflection of human nature: people like to see progress, to confirm they're headed in a sound direction. Achievement begets more achievement. A Las Vegas man said: "More people have to go out and actually accomplish stuff. I mean, it's all great and fine to sit around and talk about it and volunteer tomorrow; and volunteering is all good and fine too. But altruism can just go to a point. You want to get—you've got to get —the community *excited* about something."

It is this excitement—a belief that something meaningful is to be done *and* achieved—that will move people from where they are onto a new path. The same Las Vegas man concluded:

> I mean, right now, everybody is depressed. I know it is depression here. It's depression that nobody wants to address the problem because they're sick of the problem, and when they do voice it, no one listens.

One of the intriguing features that emerged in the various groups was that people wanted to return to the concept of things "Made in America." This is, in its implication, another feature of the pride that is a dimension of "getting back to basics." No doubt for some "Made in America" meant that the country's manufacturing base was alive and well. But many more were focusing on something quite different: how people can come together to produce in their own communities an impact that is rooted in a common purpose. As one Las Vegas man said, "Let's fix the problem—come together [and] think about what we can do to make it better."

The antidote to inaction is action. It is to no longer wait for permission from others or to believe someone else always has the best answers. A Dallas woman reached back to lessons from the founding of the nation when she said, "I think that spirit of cooperation and giving to others is what built America, because the people in the Revolutionary War weren't doing it entirely for themselves. They were doing it for a cause. And I think that Americans need a cause."

In New York City, a woman sounded a similar point about the need for a shared cause:

> I feel like everyone's looking out for themselves—the
> Republicans, the Democrats, the corporations are looking
> out for their shareholders, and there's no shared vision. I
> think that's what we need.

A Bend woman looked to the Amish as one example of people exercising a shared cause.

> Well, I think that the Amish, how they all come together to
> build a house for each other. That's the kind of philosophy
> I think [we need] as a community— you know, each
> community is a microcosm of the world.

It's worth taking a moment to underscore once more that the prescription people are setting forth here is not to be mistaken with a "small is beautiful" notion, nor "let a thousand flowers bloom," or "a thousand points of light." Not now, not with the problems they see looming across the country. The people we met believe the country faces enormous challenges that require significant action.

The purpose of starting small and starting local, and by way of this approach meeting one achievable goal after another, is to rebuild the confidence and sense of common purpose in the nation. Only then can the nation tackle its larger concerns. The message: "Let's get going! Let's set out to do things that can be achieved in the near term to get the right trajectory."

TIME COUNTS

But there's always more to this story. Kick-starting a new trajectory will always take time. As one Sonoma woman put it, "I think change is going to have to come slowly. I think it starts with every individual, actually. I think we're all responsible for that. I think Obama can only do so much. I think we have to do our part too." Or, listen to this Jacksonville woman who compared the overall challenge of moving the country in a new direction to the experience of being in debt. "You didn't get in debt overnight, and it takes time to

Simply getting going in a new direction is not enough. As a nation, we will need to pay attention long enough to ensure something real is happening over time. Otherwise, flashes of action will result in more false hope.

work your way out of it." Indeed, a Baltimore woman echoed the problem of the desire—the expectation—for instant gratification in our society. She said, "I don't think there are overnight fixes, and people in this society—like in our microwave society—always think we can just push a button and the next thing you know things are fixed. That's just not the case."

Hope requires a delicate dance between the immediate need for small actions that start local, and the longer-term commitment in which deeper changes in a country take hold.

Then, there was a New York City man who summed up many people's comments about the importance of understanding time when he said, "There seems to be a problem with maintaining a level of consistency." That is, simply getting going in a new direction is not enough. As a nation, we will need to pay attention long enough to ensure something real is happening over time. Otherwise, flashes of action will result in more false hope. Drawing on his personal experience with the aftermath of 9/11, he added:

> The difference in the temperament in the people after 9/11, it was like a different city. All of a sudden, people were holding doors for each other. Thanking police became more common. That's what affects our everyday life and does make a difference to a lot of people. I know it makes a difference to me. Why can't we maintain that type of behavior towards each other? Why is it that it barely lasted four or five months, and then the city just reverted back to the same old subwaycrowding, elbowpushing kind of mentality?… Why is it that we can't maintain that level of consistency in terms of human behavior and interaction with each other and keep it at that high level so we all can be what he [another participant] was saying, in terms of that "higher level and all getting involved and being more proactive in anything we do?" What's forcing us always to draw back?

A Denver man echoed the same observation when he said: "I think in part we're looking for inspiration to do something, like after 9/11. People liked that feeling. I remember that feeling: The patriotic feeling of wanting to do something; 'we're all in this together' kind of thing."

The hopes of both these gentleman were inextricably pinned to time. It is first about getting things moving in the right direction, then carefully and prudently building from there. It is about aptly focusing on the time and energy it actually takes to generate an authentic shift in how people see and engage with one another. This is the hope that people are telling us. It is the hope to bring about fundamental—*basic*—change. And this hope requires a delicate dance between the immediate need for small actions that start local, and the longer-term commitment in which deeper changes in a country take hold. Both are needed at this time of tumult and anxiety. Both is what is needed to create the conditions in which the nation can address its most pressing challenges. One without the other will not lead us down a new and different path.

7

THE NEW PATH FORWARD

People find their lives—and the life of this country—at a major inflection point today. We are seemingly lost inside the Tower of Babel, where the possibility for positive progress is stymied; where acrimony and divisiveness rule the day. Where, for many, fear and isolation and anxiety envelopes them, their families, even their communities. Something has to give, or else conditions will only worsen, people's frustrations will only grow. And gridlock in our public affairs surely will deepen, crowding out any remaining room to get things done.

There is no need to have to imagine these consequences; they're already happening. But choosing to go down the same old, worn path—somehow believing things will work out better if only we try harder and run faster, doing what we already do—is no longer an option. Nothing will change on that route. The pursuit of various political reforms, such as campaign finance reform or redistricting reform (just to mention two), while perhaps vitally necessary, is not the answer either—at least not in terms of what is at the heart of the concerns we are reporting. Nor, to make the point again, is the launching of a big, new shiny initiative, positioned as the magic bullet to cure our ills; or waiting for a great hero who offers up himself or herself to save us all. It is clear that no single individual, initiative, reform, or other effort, alone, can fix what must be addressed.

There is a way out of the Tower of Babel, if we focus on what matters most to people, and identify authentic ways to act on it. For this people are ready.

WHAT MATTERS

These most recent findings are *radically* different from the earlier Main Street study. So too is what it will take to put us on a different course.

The essence of what we must know is that people are expressing a profound yearning to reclaim a sense of humanity in their lives and the life of the country. Listening closely it becomes apparent they are seeking to find a door out from the Tower of Babel—any door! —to move beyond the noise that overwhelms them and to reclaim some semblance of control over their lives.

People's desire to get back to basics—the values of compassion, children, openness and humility, and concern for the common good to guide us all—is a reflection of this yearning. In the Tower of Babel, people's sense of what is good and right has come under siege, undermined at each turn, notwithstanding the many random, even planned, daily acts of kindness that people do. There is a kind of frontal assault that leaves too little room—and even less incentive—

for people to rise up and find ways to express their basic values and make them real in their own lives.

In these pages we have reported on people's desire to repudiate the "artificial" that, sadly, has become a staple of American life. We have highlighted how small and large discussions, debates and activities that purport to be rooted in authenticity and people's lives, oftentimes are untethered from people's reality, devoid of meaning and significance to them. Recall here people's concerns about misguided "self-esteem" efforts in education and youth sports; and their frustration with so-called public discourse that bears little connection to their lives. Such distortion of reality undermines people's confidence about where we are headed and sharply diminishes their attachment to matters in the public square. It's hard to feel confident when so many signals engender doubt. The fight people now seek to wage is about making our individual and collective lives more grounded in what is real, in what matters.

Many times these pages reference parents who talked about how their kids had become so enamored with online games and such that they worry about the children's ability to engage outside the home, to communicate with others, and get things done with others. Other stories tell of people trying to figure out their next move now that their job is gone, their home is underwater, or their standard of living is in jeopardy. And throughout these pages you can hear Americans say that The Golden Rule is now badly tarnished.

Perhaps in a twisted feat of irony, people report they have been active participants in producing many of the ill effects they now so desperately wish to escape—such as the rise of instant gratification at the expense of longer-term investments; a highly atomized society just when we need to come together; an American Dream that no longer seems within reach of many, in some part because too many of us overreached; and an inability to make the right decisions even when we know what they are.

People today have had enough of going it alone, being alone. Now they want to turn toward one another—not away.

People today have had enough of going it alone, being alone. Now they want to turn *toward* one another—not away.

There is something very basic that people are in search of, and it can only be created together. While going it alone is no longer an option, nor is returning to a public square echoing noise and acrimony and self-aggrandizement. There is a deep yearning to pry open a space for people, their concerns, their lives.

Reclaiming a sense of humanity is at the very essence of this study. It is about people coming back into the public square to engage with one another, to find ways to get things done together, and to restore their belief in themselves and one another. And reclaiming a sense of humanity is about seeking to tap the innate goodness and potential that already resides within each of us. For it is only by taking these actions that the negative effects now shaping the nation can be fought and, ultimately, altered. The good news is that people are raring to go—under the right conditions.

A WAY FORWARD

We know from this study that action must be taken if people are to put themselves and this nation they love on a better course. And not just any action will do—only a certain kind. In this context, striving for perfection in what is planned for or activated is not what people are seeking. Nor are they seeking efforts that offer top-down, overly linear, regimented initiatives. Surely, people's expectations will not be met by some group or organization launching yet another self-proclaimed, fool-proof recipe to change the world; or some 4-point (or 40-point!) step-by-step mega-plan to "re-create America." In our current environment, such off-base approaches will fail to meet the essence of what it means to set a new course, and of what it now takes for a path to be real in people's lives.

People want to see with clarity and confidence that we—individually and collectively—are moving in a more promising direction, a direction that offers a genuine sense of possibility and hope; one that reflects deep aspirations for themselves and for the common good. It is a path that must be believable because "belief" is the new currency of change. And along the way, people want to see proof points of progress—with one connected to others, then to many others—all adding up to a powerful, unfolding narrative that counters the negative forces that have in recent decades overtaken society. This path will need to be verifiable if it is to be believable—made clearly visible for people to see, concrete and proven over time. For only then will this new direction fully enjoy people's trust and confidence.

This means that those who lead action must be wary of tendencies to manipulate reality for their own benefit; to create flashy attempts to get Americans to "buy-in" to something "new" but which in reality is still planted on the old path; or to [even] put forth earnest hype to get people's attention, as if that will be productive in the long-term. Such efforts will not deliver the kinds of progress and results sought after here. Their only claim is to take people back to the dreadful Tower of Babel—and that's a mistake we can no longer afford. We need an approach to change that is front and center rooted in our daily activities. Otherwise we run the risk of falling back onto the well-worn path we've been on too long. Progress and hope have not been found there.

The story from Las Vegas about people's desire to paint a school together grew from sentiments that were inspiring. Yet the story was especially noteworthy because it had to do with more than just a small group of people painting a single school. Part of the larger story is that those who participated in the painting of the school could create, themselves, a new way to work together. Perhaps more important is the possible domino effect we already have described. First, children in the school being painted would see people who cared about them. Then, maybe parents of those children would decide to become more involved in their children's education, as might the surrounding community. Even more significant, people across town might see how a new and productive path forward had been created, how goals were set and achieved, so that people *could* step forward and act on something that mattered to them. This is the kind of domino effect that people want to set off, are waiting to set off. It is through these actions that new positive norms can take hold across society.

This is a way out of the Tower of Babel. Yet alone this is not enough to alter the course of people's lives—or of the nation. More is needed.

The painting of a school and other similar actions were never intended to be the answer to the nation's ills. We are all aware of the thousands upon thousands of people across the country already painting schools and such. The power of the story of painting the school is more illustrative than literal. It suggests what people are looking to achieve by coming back into the public square. People's objective is to create room and methods to make real their basic yearnings, to make concrete the possibilities for what needs to happen. These short-term efforts serve as identifiable markers for people to pursue; they shine a light on what is possible for others. They tell us that business can be done differently, together. In effect, they are vehicles by which people can take immediate, short-term actions, enabling people to get moving—now!

But even if we were to get these varied short-term, concrete actions right—and that is no small order—we must not allow ourselves to be lulled to sleep in our joy over them. Still more is needed.

We must be vigilant in connecting our short-term efforts to broader and deeper long-term actions that are required to grow and embed new and positive conditions within society. *This* is the true path people are looking for, the pay-off they wish to help create. This must be our ultimate focus. Relegating our response merely to short-term actions would be to let ourselves off the hook, merely because we can dutifully "check-off the box," showing that one group or another has painted a school, or undertaken some other recognizable effort, and then we can merrily move onto the next set of challenges on our long laundry list of "things to do." At that point, we fail. Plain and simple we will be guilty of peddling a bill of goods that cannot meet people's yearnings. That's the path we're currently on—one that people are saying we must fight against. Simply put, it is a march of folly we must avoid.

Recall, then, the other stories of people throughout these pages—the plight of men and women in the store parking lot looking for those little receipts left in abandoned shopping carts to redeem for $5, even $3; adults who are worried about children's values, their ability to apply good values in the face of adversity, and concern over who will teach them these values; families with kids in college, wondering how they will pay tuition and whether college even offers a good shot at the American Dream anymore; the individuals who feel they must steal from their helpful relatives. These trying circumstances produce enormous challenges for individual citizens. Their resolution depends on our individual and collective abilities to address them.

MAKING IT HAPPEN

To place ourselves on a more promising path will require that each of us keep front-and-center those matters that can easily slip from our minds as we engage in our daily activities. At issue is how to reclaim the necessary space in our lives for authentic human interactions to occur, for people to come together, and for seeds of belief to be nurtured and grown.

Here are five ways to meet people where they are and to help them express their deepest yearnings. These five approaches are not intended to be exhaustive, nor comprehensive. They offer starting points for us all. They are reminders—even better, action items— and each one is laid out in juxtaposition to an assumption that oftentimes drives our present-day actions—a kind of conventional wisdom, if you will. This is not meant to diminish or dismiss such assumptions, but to acknowledge them and to demonstrate the kinds of underlying tensions that exist between them and a new path forward. In fact, it is by revealing these tensions—indeed, by engaging them—that progress will be made. After all, if the answers to our challenges were so easy or already known we would have put them in place by now. But reality shifts, conditions change, new challenges confront us: how we respond is always at issue. Whatever ultimate actions we take, these five approaches will be helpful guides. For progress comes when we engage our often unexamined assumptions, when we place competing ideas and solutions on the table and genuinely try to make sense of their value, given the challenges at hand, as we seek to sort out the direction that is most relevant at this time. This kind of generative approach is at the heart of creating a new way forward.

Here, then, are five ways to find and make real a path forward.

First, we *do* need "fast and easy" ways for people to engage with one another in the public square. Indeed, there is rapid growth among groups and organizations offering a whole host of so-called "fast and easy" ways for people to volunteer for a quick 30-minute activity, oftentimes on their own or to donate money online or via text to a favorite cause. Without such convenience, the argument goes, people will not step forward, possibly never engaging at all. There is, I believe, some truth in this. There is always a need for people to have different pathways into public life to express their passions. But at issue here is more than the "fast and easy."

We must know that people want to forge real connections *with* each other—between and among themselves—connections that provide possibility for building extended trust and new norms. It's not that fast and easy engagement is wrong; but it simply may skate over what's truly at issue. People are seeking a change in the very nature and quality of our relationships. So our task now is to avoid succumbing primarily to fast and easy ways of engagement as the answer to people's deep yearnings. We need to make the necessary room for people to come back into the public square in ways that ensure they are *with* one another—interacting, building trust.

Second, we *do* need "big impact" solutions, for tremendous, seemingly intractable problems do persist in communities and must be addressed. There are big audacious goals—like reducing the high school drop-out rate—that can help people focus on such matters and rally around a common endeavor.

But such efforts also can miss a pivotal point in our way to a new path. As we have seen, people want to start by taking small, local actions, for it is on such paths that people may come out from their homes and get things done *together*, in ways that are achievable, do-able, where they can get their arms around the actions and goals they want to pursue. This is the *human scale* on which people now want to act—where they can see and hear one another, do things together, and activate their sense of humanity.

This is important and vital: people want to do things close to home, so they can believe in something because they can see and drive it together. Our task then is to produce opportunities for people to act on a human scale. Small and local is where people want to start—where they can regain their footing, confidence, and ability to do things together. Of course, the danger here is to say one is pursuing this new path but fail to authentically operate at the human scale.

Third, we *do* need "efficiency." After all, a hallmark of America is to strive to do things faster, bigger, and with fewer or limited or more efficient resources! But there is nothing efficient about people's yearning to "get back to basics"—for instance, to ignite a greater sense of compassion, to exhibit greater openness and humility, and the recognition of a common good in society. There's the rub. People need real room where the give-and-take of compassion can flourish; where they can feel safe in being open to different ideas and perspectives; where there is a focus on the common good, not just people's own good.

Getting back to basics through the exercise of these enduring values is what makes for a good society. And this is what people are in search of. When such space has been squeezed out of society, we forfeit the basic opportunity for society to work. Our task then is to be ever-vigilant in how we approach this path forward. It is all too easy to adopt these words—*compassion, openness, humility,* and the *common good*—but not their true meaning. We must create, in various initiatives and efforts in our own lives, the room for these enduring values to be exercised and to flourish. This only can happen over time.

Fourth, we also need new "systems." A systemic approach is required to transform schools that are failing our school children—and to address a whole host of other challenges. To make progress demands a collective action: to generate the public will to act, to marshal necessary resources, and to engage in productive public discourse. These efforts, among others, require a shared determination. And at the root of collective action is the need for people to restore their belief in themselves, and in one another, to believe that such action is possible. Being clear, promoting trust and confidence, operating at a human scale, getting back to basics—all these must be tended to if collective action is to work.

But without this underlying foundation, collective action is neither doable nor sustainable—as we've seen in too many communities, and in the nation itself. Our task then is to actively cultivate people's desire to develop trust and confidence, operate on a human scale, and get back to basics, and to do this when working on specific issues. Otherwise, dreams of collective action become more like nightmares in the Tower of Babel.

Fifth, it is true the country must "change direction," but there's no way to take a country of more than 300 million people and flip a switch, as if change will come that easily or swiftly. Nor is there any way to tear down the Tower of Babel in a day. The good news is that people do not harbor such expectations. What gives people hope is to know we are moving in a better direction, down the right path. Recognition of this new direction comes about by people seeing that different, seemingly disparate actions are tied together, that they add up to something larger than just themselves, constituting a genuinely different direction from the current path. This requires real proof points and radically different communications. Rather than view each action that people, groups, and organizations take as an isolated event, or even a collection of isolated events (as if they alone are all that is needed to change direction), we must view them in a broader context. Moreover, it will not be enough for people, groups, and organizations to promote only their own actions—as if they alone will constitute the new path. It is only when individual actions become connected to a larger, unfolding narrative, when they serve as proof points in a larger story, they gain meaning and create a renewed sense of possibility.

Thus, whether in a neighborhood, community, or the country as a whole, we must create this new narrative by weaving together a story made up of seemingly disparate points, which in reality are very much connected.

Our task then is to know that "change" won't come all at once—it never has. To inspire us, along the path ahead, we must create a new narrative about being on a better course, one that offers genuine hope. This happens when we "connect the dots" for people—so they can see how one proof point of real action connects to another—and *many* others. Coherence and meaning are essential to people gaining a new sense of possibility.

MAKING OUR WAY

The actions laid out here know no domain or boundaries. They apply to leaders of all stripes, organizations of all kinds, and communities of all sizes. They apply to everyone. These actions are not simply *nice* to do, but *necessary* if we are to *hear* and *see* one another. If we are to figure out ways to act on common challenges we face. If we are to marshal our resources of money, time, and talent to make a

To inspire us, along the path ahead, we must create a new narrative about being on a better course, one that offers genuine hope.

real difference, and if we are to generate the public will for sustainable action. When we move in these ways people can exercise greater control over their own lives, the communities in which they live, and the nation as a whole.

Of course, none of the actions noted here can by themselves "solve" the challenges that confront us; but without these actions we cannot effectively move forward as a society. We are stuck and stymied, with too many people feeling left isolated and alone, many even bereft of possibility. But as we have come to know from these discussions across the country, to make this forward movement more possible, we must make room within people's lives and the larger society for a greater sense of humanity. We must act on a more human scale. We must ignite a greater degree of compassion, openness, and humility and further the common good. And we must restore people's belief in themselves and one another. *These* yearnings we must know—and act on—if we wish to make our way forward.

APPENDIX

Methodology

The Harwood Institute used focus groups—or group discussions—to conduct this study. These are an ideal research method for this type of endeavor. They provide citizens with the opportunity to think about various issues and topics over the course of a discussion of several hours, to talk about their views and feelings in their own words, and to describe the underlying assumptions behind their views. Moreover this research approach helps to identify the language that citizens use to talk about specific topics; and focus groups allow citizens to react to new information and proposals during the course of a discussion. Such interaction is difficult—often impossible—to obtain through public opinion surveys.

There are, of course, limitations to group discussions. The research is qualitative. Thus, the observations detailed in this report should not be mistaken for findings from a random sample survey. They are, technically speaking, hypotheses, or insights, that would need to be validated by reliable quantitative methods before being considered definitive. Still, the insights are strongly suggestive of how citizens view politics, their communities, and their relationship to both.

Each of the group discussions conducted for this study comprised approximately 12-15 people, representing a cross-section of age, race, income, education, and party affiliation. The participants were recruited by a professional public opinion research firm in each location. Each group meeting lasted for about three hours and was led by a trained moderator and recorded. Participants were promised that their names would not appear in this report, in order to respect their privacy.

To ensure geographic diversity in this study, 11 discussion groups were conducted across the nation. Eight were held in the following communities during 2011:

LOCATION	DATE
Detroit, Michigan	May 26
Champaign-Urbana, Illinois	June 7
Sonoma, California	July 25
Bend, Oregon	July 27
Jacksonville, Florida	August 25
Las Vegas, Nevada	September 15
New York, New York	September 28
Dallas, Texas	October 17

Three additional discussion groups were held in 2012 to further test and update the results. The findings from these groups mirrored those from the earlier conversations. The additional groups were held in:

Nashville, Tennessee	March 12
Baltimore, Maryland	March 13
Denver, Colorado	March 19

ACKNOWLEDGMENTS

There are many people to thank who helped make this book possible.

I am indebted to David Mathews, president of the Kettering Foundation. For nearly 25 years, he has partnered with the Harwood Institute for Public Innovation, providing inspiration and guidance and new ways to think about public life and politics.

Also at the Kettering Foundation, I wish to thank John Dedrick, vice president and director of programs, and Deborah Witte, program officer, who made this study and its publication possible. Both have been wonderful and cherished partners in our long-term work together. And Lisa Boone-Berry, copy editor for the foundation, put her fine touches on the manuscript.

There is the team at the Harwood Institute to thank. Aaron Leavy, senior manager for learning and innovation, spent countless hours with me on the study's design and implementation and in discussing the results; he is a wise and trusted partner. In addition, Jennifer Barton, our operations director; Jim Cooney, the communications manager; Alisa Silverman; and Melissa Eastham, all helped move this study to its fruition. And I want to thank John Creighton, who led some of the group discussions; John and I have been working together for nearly 20 years.

I want to thank Harris Dienstfrey, who took time out from his busy schedule to help me complete this book. His suggestions and insights are always wonderful and always strengthen the final product.

I saved the last word for my editor, Robert J. Kingston. We have been collaborating for my entire work-life, starting some 30 years ago. He edited the first Main Street study, *Citizens and Politics*; and now, he edited *The Work of Hope* (and many pieces in-between!). It is something special when your editor fully understands your approach to writing, to making an argument, and to the use of language helping you strengthen, even transform, what you have to say. Perhaps the greatest gift of working on this latest piece has been the opportunity to team up with Bob again.

ABOUT THE AUTHOR

Richard C. Harwood is founder and president of The Harwood Institute for Public Innovation, a nonprofit, catalytic organization dedicated to helping people find new pathways to imagine and act for the public good. For nearly two decades, Harwood has led the charge to redeem hope in public life and politics, discovering how to create change in the face of negative conditions. He has developed new kinds of public innovators and civic-minded organizations in dozens of communities across the country. Harwood has devoted his energies to spreading a vision for what American society should be and putting innovative practices to use on the ground to turn that vision into reality. Among his many publications, he is author of *Hope Unraveled: The People's Retreat and Our Way Back* (Kettering Foundation Press, 2005) and *Make Hope Real* (Kettering Foundation, 2007).

People seek to kick-start a new direction for the
country, a new sense of hope and possibility.

To learn more about what you can do, subscribe
the Rich's blog at
www.theharwoodinstitute.org/blog
then visit
www.theharwoodinstitute.org